BLUEJACKET LEGACY

BLUEJACKET LEGACY

When One Defining Moment Shapes a Life

JULIE BOYD and DR. EILEEN LOCKHART

Charleston, SC

www.PalmettoPublishing.com

Bluejacket Legacy:
When One Defining Moment Shapes a Life

First Edition

Paperback ISBN: 978-1-68515-084-6

eBook ISBN: 978-1-68515-085-3

Table of Contents

Introduction

*The hardest struggle of all is to be something different
from what the average man is.*

Robert H. Schuller

Many years ago, our father gave each of his children
a series of tapes on which he recorded the story of
his life. When he gave us these tapes, we were all in
the throes of raising children, building our careers, and
generally being consumed with the daily tasks of simply
living. We listened to the tapes as we had time but never
really listened to them. Several years ago, my sister and
I developed a keen interest in our father's ancestry. We
researched and traveled to discover our roots. Slowly,
along our journey, my sister and I would often wonder
how our father fit into the big picture. We learned how
stoic our grandfather was and how important family dy-
namics were to him. Seeing these same traits exhibited
by our father, we wanted to learn more about how these
same traits were instilled in him. We decided to pull out
the dusty tapes and begin to listen and transcribe them
on paper. We soon discovered this was not any easy task.
There were seven full cassette tapes. The first tape reminded us of all the home movies we were required to
watch about airplanes and navy hangers…monotonous!

1

Unfortunately, our father did not have any stories to re-call about this early period of his life, so we laboriously listened to newspaper accounts of happenings in the ear-ly 1920s.

Once we managed to transcribe the first half of that first tape, we were slowly beginning to form a picture of a man we never knew. Every sibling has their own perspective of the relationship they shared with a parent. My sister and I discovered we both had a very similar in-terpretation of our experiences with our father. He never talked about life before he was our father. So, we never knew or wondered what he was like as a child or young man. To us, he was stoic, and neither of us were close to him. He was the "wait until your father gets home" type of father. He was not an easy man to love, and there were periods in our lives when we disliked him. One time when my sister and I were talking about this book, we both shared the fact that we could not go into a card shop and easily pick out a card to fit our feelings. Our chosen cards seemed to be almost generic. Sad.

Writing this joint project gave us true insight into the mind of our father. We learned that he was trying to build a better family than he had growing up. He was following the path of his generation by working hard and providing more than he had as a child. Our family rules and firm discipline were examples of values he learned as a child.

This book is one sailor's story of growing up during the Great Depression, surviving Pearl Harbor, and build-ing a career in the Jet Age.

Prologue

Dying was nothing and he had no picture of it nor fear of it in his mind. But living was a field of grain blowing in the wind on the side of a hill. Living was a hawk in the sky.

Ernest Hemingway

Sitting in the shower Bob closed his eyes and let the shower spray fall over him. He knew he had a fever and thought a warm shower would ease it away. It had been several weeks since he first was sick. He believed it was the flu, but the muscle aches, dizziness, and blackouts were getting to be too much to handle, and he just could not shake this bug. Afterall, he was 89 years old. The shower water began to cool, and he looked up to see his wife reach into the shower and turn off the water. He turned his head upward and glanced at the shower window. He saw the torn screen and a few mosquitos flying in and out of the window. He thought to himself, *I really need to move the water bucket away from the window. Standing water just breeds those things and they are so big.* He scratched a bug bite on his arm. The sounds around him faded and went black.

He began to wake up as someone was shaking him. The arms were strong and gently lifted him out of the shower. Many thoughts raced through his mind. He was disoriented, not knowing where he was or what day it was. He wondered if he was wounded. Memories flooded his thoughts. *This must be what it is like when you're dying. What is that noise? It's the siren again, the air raid siren. It's so dark. No, it's not dark. It can't be dark. It's daytime. It is the smoke, so much smoke and loud...people running. I don't want to look.*

"Bob Barrigan? Mr. Barrigan, can you hear me?"

"Mr. Barrigan, I am here to help you. Can you open your eyes?"

Bob does not move. In his mind he answers and questions what is happening. *No, I don't want to open my eyes. Where am I? Am I hit? Am I dying? I think I'm dying.*

A soft female voice whispers, "Bob, can you hear me? I'm right here. This young man is just here to help. You need to cooperate with him." The voice continues as she takes his hand. "These men are here to take you to the hospital. They are EMTs."

"No!" Bob's voice weakly croaks with a mixture of force and quiet desperation. He squeezes his eyes tight and then opens them. "I don't want to go to the hospital. If I go, I will never come out."

"That's not true, Mr. Barrigan. The hospital can help you. My friends and I are going to take you in the ambulance, but you need to have some clothes on. You're naked. Let me help you put some pants on."

The EMT reaches for his arms, and Bob lets him dress him. Bob begins to slip back into his memories. He slumps, thinking *I'm so tired. It's hard to keep fighting.*

I'm naked? I'd left my uniform in my room with my rifle. I didn't need it while I was working on the plane, and then I heard the sirens. I couldn't make it back to barracks before the first bomb lit up the sky.

Bob's thoughts are interrupted. "Mr. Barrigan, we're going to carry you to the ambulance. You're a WWII vet and a Pearl Harbor survivor too! I understand you have some medals. Thank you for your service to our country. I'm proud of you. I want you to know that. We're all proud of you. I need to you to hang in there for a little while longer. I know you're tough, right? You know that too," the EMT keeps talking.

Several on the EMT's medical team lift and strap Bob to a gurney for the ambulance. Bob's eyes are tightly closed. He feels the cold as a draft curl around his toes. He feels sick to his stomach. He questions going to the hospital.

"I hate the hospital. It smells like chicken," he says and the EMT pats his arm. Bob remembers the day after the bombing when he walked into the mess hall. They were serving chicken and all the dead bodies laid in the mess hall.

"Mr. Barrigan, what are you saying about chicken?" someone asks.

Bob shivers. He grimaces and says to himself; *I'm not opening my eyes again. I hear the sirens and the planes. They're coming back. I can feel it. This is what it feels like to die.* He sighs and thinks of his home where he grew up in California. His mother and father, Raul and Jessie, flash before his eyes. He can see them clearly, like they were when he was a boy. Will I see them again when I die? What is it they say? Your life flashes before your eyes? Bob feels himself drifting away and he doesn't have the strength to fight it.

Chapter 1

In every conceivable manner, the family is a link to our past.
Bridge to our future.

Alex Haley

Raul Barrigan looked across the audience to find her face. She always sat in the first row. The room was dimly lit, but it didn't really matter. He could always pick out her smile and the curve of her neck, and oh, how her eyes sparkled when the screen lit up. It would be glamorous to say Raul and Jessie met on the set of a silent film stage, but Raul was a projectionist at the King Rama Theater in Alhambra, Los Angeles, and Jessie frequently came to the theater to watch the silent films.

While sitting in the little booth running the reels, Raul would often gaze down and study the moviegoers. One afternoon, he spied Jessie in the crowd. From his view, she appeared to be poised, colorfully dressed, and appealing in a ruffled sort of way. He noticed that when she laughed at the screen, her entire face lit up as though she was lit from within. With a growing sense of interest, Raul began to search for her in the crowd each week. One afternoon, Jessie arrived at the movies to see *The Fury*, starring Richard Barthelmess and Lillian Gish. Raul decided to quickly make his move right after the show. He darted out of his booth and over to Jessie to introduce himself and ask her to dinner.

Wooing Jessie was easy for Raul. He was an attractive man with the classic good looks of actors of that time; he was often compared to a young Groucho Marx with his dark looks, bushy eyebrows, and luminous dark eyes. He had a wiry build and black curly hair that met in a dramatic widow's peak on his forehead. Born in Tucson, Arizona, to parents of Greek and Native American heritage, he was a gentleman with a serious nature. There was also a sense of understated power that surrounded him.

Jessie had waves of hair that tumbled to her shoulders. Her hair was dark and silky and reflected her personality. She was a strong-willed woman and loved life. She was accustomed to change. When Jessie was young, she traveled to California with her mother, Eva, and older brother, Freddy. Once, before moving to California, she and Freddy were abandoned in an orphanage because their mother had remarried, and her second husband did not want children. Eventually her mother's new husband grew bored and left Eva. As soon as he was out of the picture, Eva collected Jessie and Freddy and moved to settle in Los Angeles.

Jessie and Raul's relationship grew after their first date. They both shared the characteristics of energy and hard work; however, their commonalities stopped there. Jessie was a dreamer. She filled her days with work, music, and the arts. This is what first attracted Raul. She sang and wrote songs, painted, and found numerous outlets for her creativity. Raul, on the other hand, began his career in the film industry as a teen in Tucson, Arizona, and believed in hard work first. In those days, he left little time for entertainment and fun. Although sharing the same basic values, Raul and Jessie were drawn to each other despite their differences. This is not always the prediction of a good marriage. Nevertheless, they married in the early 1920s and settled in Pico Heights, a small neighborhood of working-class immigrants and blue-collar workers in Los Angeles.

Jessie and Raul's oldest child, Robert, was born in January of 1923. Jessie doted on her first child and fondly called him Bobby. Motherhood was good for her. Working for neighbors, mending or washing clothes, she delighted in the time she could spend with her new son. Raul, still working at the movie theater, put in long hours to make ends meet. These were hard times, but harder times were in their future.

World War I was over, and people were trying to get their feet back on the ground. Even though America was starting to grow, as it did after every war, growth was extremely slow in the dry dusty areas of Southern California. When Jessie became pregnant with their second child, Raul decided the small family should move to Calexico, California. Calexico is a small border town in the Imperial Valley that lies in the southern desert of California.

Raul always had a penchant for cars, and America was the land of the automobile! He bought an old Ford

Model T for the family to make the trip to Calexico. Some people called the car the Tin Lizzie since it was cheaply made and a cheaply priced automobile. The car had to be hand cranked to start, and gas had to be ordered from the drugstore. Since the trip would take them through the desert, much planning went into their preparations. No matter how much you prepare, there are always stones along the way. At this time there were no paved roads, so the family had to follow the emigrant route to Southern California. Travel was slow, sweaty, and dusty. Sleeping outside of their car at night gave them little escape from the relentless daily heat.

During the trek into the desert, their car broke down in the middle of the day. Raul planned to replenish their supplies, especially their water, in the next small town. Although he was resourceful and packed what he thought he might need on the journey, their water supply was getting low. He had everything he needed to fix the car, but it would take some time. As the afternoon wore on, Raul found fixing the car was much more difficult than he imagined. Soon, his work dragged into the night. By morning, their supply of water ran out, and Jessie was frantic about the baby. Little Bobby, almost one years old, developed a cough during the dusty trip and was sweaty and feverish. Raul continued to work on the car while Jessie sang to Bobby and prayed for a miracle.

Midmorning, they saw dust stirring in the distance. Dust meant a vehicle and people. It wasn't too long before a rickety truck came upon them. The driver was a weathered old Mexican man headed to Los Angeles with a truck bed full of watermelons! Prayers had been answered, the truck was fixed, and baby Bobby feasted on watermelon juice.

When they finally reached Calexico, Raul rented a small house, and Jessie began to prepare for the birth of her second child. Bobby was barely two when Lucille was born. Bobby was a stocky toddler with a mop of black curly hair. He inherited his father's widow peak and dark looks. Bobby's days with his mother were filled with songs, music, and work. When his father returned from a day of work, the house quieted. Raul felt he was the provider for the family and set high expectations for his wife and child. Raul expected Jessie to stay home and keep the house and take good care of Bobby. He did not want his wife to work outside of the home and expected her to defer to him in all matters.

The following two years brought two more children, Raul Jr., and George. Even with four children under five, Jessie still maintained her spirit and love for her children. She instilled a strong work ethic in them at an early age.

Since Bobby was the oldest, he was usually assigned the more difficult tasks. One of his chores was to scrub the wooden floors of the house. There were vacuum cleaners in the catalogs, but only for houses with rugs. Also, vacuums were not electric. They had to be pushed hard to force the dirt up into the canister. Bobby's family did not have to worry about that problem; their house had all wooden floors. Bobby's house had a large living room. Each week, he and Lucille were required to scrub the floor with stiff brushes. Even at five, Bobby always looked for ways to make his work more entertaining for himself and his sister.

"Lucille! Go grab the soap and brushes, and I will get some buckets and water," hollered Bobby.

"The brushes are heavy, Bobby," complained Lucille.

Running out the door, Bobby called, "Just do it. It will be fun!"

Supplies gathered; Bobby demonstrated to Lucille how to fill their stiff brushes with soap.

"Ready, Lucille? Follow me!" Bobby gleefully told her.

Bobby began to quickly slide across the floor, sitting on one of the large brushes. Lucille jumped in, and the entire floor was hastily covered with large soapy bubbles. Hearing the squeals of the children appearing to be having too much fun scrubbing the floor, Jessie appeared in the doorway with hands on hips and a frown on her face.

"Bobby! What a mess you have made! You and Lucille need to quickly clean up this soapy water all over the floor so it can dry before your father comes home," sternly scolded Jessie.

Bobby and Lucille, downcast and chastised, replied in unison, "Yes, Mama."

Jessie returned to the kitchen with a secret smile on her face, thinking about the ingenuity of her two small children.

During this time, Raul was trying to support his family on his income alone. Jessie brought in a little money by washing and cleaning for some neighbors, but the main responsibility of support fell to Raul. As the country headed toward the Great Depression, jobs became sparser. Movie theaters began to close because many people simply could not afford that luxury. Raul had not yet joined the union because it was not in place in Calexico in the mid-1920s. When his theater closed, he was forced to search elsewhere for work. Raul was discouraged, but he also knew he was resourceful. He always found a job. It may have been menial, but he did support his family when the theaters closed. They were poor, but Bobby, at his young age, never realized it. He accepted the fact that he worked hard at five years old and never questioned it. He was happy. Bobby knew his mother loved him beyond a doubt and his father loved him in a way he could not yet understand.

Chapter 2

It is easier to build strong children than to repair broken men.

Frederick Douglas

Religion was one area where Raul and Jessie disagreed. Raul was a Catholic, and Jessie was brought up loosely as a Methodist. They both wanted the children to attend church, but they could not agree on which church. The couple argued endlessly on this topic. Jessie knew that Raul would win in the end. He always did. But she wanted him to know how strongly she felt about the decision and held out as long as she could. Raul ended up taking the children with him to church on Sundays while Jessie occasionally attended the local Protestant church.

The family was growing quickly, and there was always another baby to feed and care for. Jessie continued to stay home and care for her children. Raul found work with another movie theater nearby. He had experience, so the pay was fair, but it was still a struggle to provide for his family. Sometimes he would find extra work as a mechanic around the town. When Bobby was five, Jessie discovered she was pregnant with twins. Soon, there would be six children under the age of six to care for.

As the time for the birth of the twins drew near, it was also time for Bobby to be baptized. One Sunday afternoon, Raul walked Bobby to the large stone Catholic church in town. Raul stood beside his son while the priest baptized him. It was a solemn time, and both Bobby and Raul were quiet as they slowly walked home. Bobby's parents were somber that evening. He noticed there no stories, and his mother was subdued.

Early the next morning, Jessie came into Bobby's room, which he shared with his siblings, and told him to get dressed because she and his father were going to take a walk. Bobby was excited that he was going on a walk with his parents. He quickly dressed and met them at the door. He walked between his parents, holding his mother's hand. They walked down the street to the Catholic school and started toward the entrance.

"Bobby," Jessie said quietly, "your father and I are going to leave you here at the school for a while."

Bobby tried to process what his mother had said. Leave him? For how long was he to stay at the school? He thought they might have errands to do, and he would be in the way. There was no opportunity to ask his parents because they were already walking up to the large wooden door. After they entered the echoing hall with a tall domed ceiling, a nun walked quietly out of the shadows and welcomed them. Jessie pried Bobby's hand from hers and turned and walked away, following Raul to the door. Neither parent looked back or uttered a word to Bobby.

Bobby, five years old, felt abandoned and bewildered. He was motionless and so brokenhearted that he started quietly sobbing. The nun gently took Bobby's hand and led him into a small chapel and up to a statue of Jesus. She encouraged Bobby to kneel with her. Putting an arm around Bobby, she let him cry until his tears finally dried and he was left with only hiccups. The nun explained to Bobby that he would live at the school for a while and learn many new things. She assured him that someday his parents would come back and get him. Booby didn't know if he believed her because he felt so forlorn. He managed a slight nod and followed the nun.

Children are resilient and learn to adapt. Bobby was sad, but he became accustomed to the new daily routine. He made friends, had plenty to eat, and the nuns were kind to him. Many of his days were spent sitting in small chairs at long tables as he learned to write cursive handwriting. The nuns would come to him as he sat, placing their large hands over his as he made goose eggs, large oval circles. He waited, hoping that his parents would come back soon. He was really missing his parents and his sisters and brothers.

Just like the nun told him the first day, his parents did come back for him. Six weeks later, they showed up and took him across the street to the public school where he was enrolled in kindergarten. His parents left him there for the day with instructions to walk home after school. When Bobby arrived at home late in the afternoon, he discovered he had a new brother and sister! Bobby's parents never told him why he was sent away from home. He never asked.

Bobby thrived in kindergarten. He was drawn to all the paper projects they worked on in class. He prized the time he spent creating designs, using scissors, coloring, and pasting. Unfortunately, one day when Bobby was hard at work on a project with his scissors, he vaguely noticed his teacher bending over in front of him to help another child with their work. Not really thinking but gazing at the beautiful flowery pattern in front of him, he used his scissors to follow the pattern up the back of her dress.

"Bobby!" cried the teacher. "What have you done?"

Looking up at her, he realized he had snipped her dress all the way up the skirt!

Mortified, Bobby flung the scissors out of his hand and mumbled, "I am sorry."

Bobby's parents were called, and his mother soon arrived to take him home. Jessie scolded him all the way home. He was a little worried about what his father would say when he found out. Bobby knew that he did not do it on purpose, but no one would believe him, and he really couldn't understand why he did it. Raul was angry with Bobby, but other than asking a few questions, Raul remained stern and quiet. He told Bobby to go outside to the car. Now, Bobby was worried that he was being taken back to the Catholic school church. Once outside, he saw his father motioning him to the trunk of the car. Over the trunk is where Bobby received his first spanking. Humiliated more than any physical pain, Bobby quietly took his punishment and vowed never to have to repeat it. That was a promise a five-year-old would find hard to keep.

1929 and 1930 were especially difficult years for Bobby's family. The stock market crashed, and thousands of people were out of jobs. Since Bobby's family was already poor, the children did not experience any difference in their daily lives. Raul still had his job at the theater, and he had also joined the labor union. But now there were seven children in the family. Jessie had just given birth to a daughter.

Holidays in the family were observed, but the children did not always receive gifts. Raul always managed to find a tree somewhere and bring it home so Jessie and the children could decorate the Christmas tree with their handmade creations. If it had been a good year, the children might receive a present. Bobby received two special presents from his father in 1929 and 1930. One of the presents was a bright red fire engine with a siren and long ladders. It had a handle on it and lots of hoses. Bobby would fill the tank with water and squirt the water out through the hoses. He loved squirting his siblings and watching them scatter and squeal. The older ones never fled to Jessie. They knew how busy their mother was with the babies.

Bobby's second present from his father was a tricycle. It was a hand-me-down from a friend of his father's. He loved the tricycle until his mother made him take it outside. He tried unsuccessfully to ride it around his yard. The yard was made of rocks and sand, so he didn't get very far in the dirt. There were many times he tried to ride it out of the yard and on to the road, but his mother always seemed to catch him and herd him back into the yard.

Most evenings, after chores had been finished, Bobby would join the other boys and girls on the block in a hodgepodge of games. Sometimes, they played hockey with a tin can, forming boisterous teams. If they found a big old tire, they would take turns crawling into the middle of the tire while someone pushed them around the block. Sometimes they would trade milk bottles and soda caps. The boys collected all kinds of caps from beer bottles, soda pop; the most favorite being birch beer, lemon drop soda, cherry blossom soda and wink. Taking the cork out from under the cap, the boys would put the cork under their shirts and push the caps onto it. They would proudly strut around with all the caps on their shirts. Playing cowboys was also a favorite game. They would make their own pistols and rifles out of clothespins, cardboard, and rubber tubes. The boys would line up and take turns having a shootout with other or chase the girls around, shooting at them.

When Bobby was around seven, he started selling *Liberty* magazines. This was his first official job outside of the home. Of course, he still had to do his chores. He had a regular route with about thirty magazine subscriptions. He walked all over the neighborhood delivering papers and collecting the money.

Sometimes he sold little black silhouettes his mother had made. Jessie drew and cut out silhouettes and placed each one on tin foil to make them stand out. He sold these for fifteen cents, and they were popular around the town.

Bobby met a few unusual characters during his route. One day, he saw one of his customers at the grocery store lugging a large bag of fruit and vegetables home. She was a stooped older woman who lived alone in a small adobe house off the alley where he lived.

Bobby offered eagerly, "Would you like me to carry that bag home for you?"

The woman gave him an enthusiastic smile and handed the groceries to him. While the two walked to her home, they struck up a conversation, mostly the old woman talking and Bobby listening. Once they arrived home and Bobby had placed the groceries in the kitchen, the old woman offered to show him around her place. The woman was touched by his interest in all of the old things around her house. Bobby noticed a Victrola in her living room with a picture of Rudolf Valentino, a popular Hollywood Latino actor, sitting on top of it in a shiny frame. Noticing Bobby's interest in the picture, the old woman told Bobby that she was Rudolf Valentino's mother. Bobby sat for several hours, enthralled by her stories of her son. Walking home, Bobby wondered if her stories were true. As a young impressionable boy, he decided to believe her.

On another occasion, when Bobby was going door to door selling magazines, he went to a tenement house in a poor neighborhood he had not been to before. Bobby knocked on the door. A tall, beautiful lady wearing lots of makeup and a flouncy purple boa round her neck answered the knock.

After gazing at her a moment with wide eyes, he stammered, "Would you like to buy a *Liberty* magazine, lady?"

The lady kindly answered, "Of course I will buy a magazine, sonny."

From inside the house, Bobby heard a woman holler, "Find out if he will take it out in trade."

Bobby was confused and did not know how to answer. Before he could think of a response, the lady handed him the money and thanked him. Bobby wondered about this incident all the way home. The woman sure was pretty. He recounted the story to his mother, asking what was meant by "taking it out in trade." The only response Bobby received from his mother was that there were some apartment houses that were not ones for children to be knocking on the door!

Bobby carried his love of school into his mid elementary years. Because they were poor and they lived in the desert where it was very hot, Bobby and his siblings did not wear shoes to school. In the winter months, when the weather was a little milder, he wore twill cotton pants, a button-down shirt, and Buster Brown shoes. Clothes were scarce for the children. There were many, many hand-me-downs and lots of washings.

Jessie would pack the children's lunches in little brown paper bags. Lunch was simple. It usually consisted of an egg or tomato sandwich, an apple or celery, and a little glass jar of milk. One day, when Bobby was in the third grade, he arrived at school before the bell rang. He ran to play with some of his friends on the merry-go-round. He was laughing and spinning, all the while clutching his brown lunch bag in his hand. Suddenly, the cap popped off the milk bottle and soaked his lunch. He started crying so hard the teacher came out in the schoolyard to see what had happened to him. He was not physically hurt, and he wasn't even crying because he had no lunch. Bobby was crying because he knew how hard his mother worked to scrape food together for their lunches. Bobby felt so bad.

The culture of the day made an impression on Bobby. He had three passions in his lifetime: films, music, and airplanes. His love of films certainly was attributed to his father's profession. Bobby loved the movies! Douglass Fairbanks, Buster Keaton, and Lillian Gish were just a few of the actors and actresses he loved.

Every time a new movie came out, the theater used to hold contests. Sometimes the manager would ask a group of children to come up on stage and compete against each other. Competitions were always fun. Sometimes they competed in barrel races on stage or who best imitated a silly walk like Charlie Chaplin, a famous silent film comedian that strutted like a penguin. Raul always warned his children not to go on stage because he was an employee of the theater. Sometimes, Bobby could not resist, and the manager always egged Bobby to come on stage and participate. The manager had a soft spot for Raul's children and frequently did something special for them.

One time when the Tarzan movies began to come out, Bobby was called to the stage. Even knowing his father would most likely be mad later, Bobby scampered onto the stage with a group of other boys. The boys were each given a leotard and told to go backstage. Once backstage, they had to take off their clothes and put on the leotard. They were then given a leopard drape to throw over their shoulders. Going back in front of the audience, they were told to take big leaps and holler the best Tarzan yell they could. Even though Bobby was very shy when he was young, he took his best leaps and gave his best yells. Bobby didn't win, but he was proud of himself that he tried. His father was not so happy. Raul was angry at Bobby and gave him a good yelling at after returning home after work. Bobby was surprised he did not get the spanking he was expecting. Later that evening, Raul confessed to Jessie that he was pleased Bobby had shown some spunk and went up on the stage. After that incident, Bobby could participate in some of the contests. Sometimes he won, but most times he didn't.

For a second time the theaters closed. There were not enough people who could afford the ten cents for the movies. People always knew life would get better and the theaters would reopen. After a long dry spell, the shows reopened, and the managers would offer something to entice the people back. The manager would hold what they called bank nights. The cartoons and newsreels would run, and then the manager would stop the show right before the feature started. Someone would roll out a barrel filled with ticket stubs. The manager would choose a stub from the barrel, and the lucky person would win a bag of groceries, oatmeal boxes, or dishes. Jessie loved these evenings. She always went.

Even though Raul would tell Jessie not to go because employees were not supposed to engage in these contests, she ignored him. By this time, Jessie and Raul had nine children, and Jessie had no time for the things she once considered fun. Devoted to her children, she still yearned for some excitement and something different in her life. Jessie and Raul began to drift apart.

Bobby's second passion, music, came from Jessie. There was usually sometime during the day before Raul came home for Jessie to share her love of music with her children. The family had a large mahogany Victrola that was kept in the living room. Bobby was already devoted to the radio and loved to listen to songs like "Sonny Boy," "Around My Shoulder," and "Don't Sit under the Apple Tree." Now, with the Victrola, he found himself dipping his head under it to attempt to place his head inside the box, trying to listen to the music. Jessie frequently found him that way and would always giggle when she saw his chubby legs sticking out from under the box. Bobby claimed his favorite singer was Al Jolson, and thus began his love of big band music.

Raul would sometimes take the children to airshows near the Imperial Airport near El Centro. Sometimes there were wing walkers on the airplanes. These men and women daredevils would climb out on to the plane's wings while the airplane was in the air. Bobby considered these wing walkers to be above all else. He would watch them in awe as they climbed on the wings while the planes dipped down toward the crowd and the walkers grabbed little yellow flags that were attached to a wire strung between two poles. He loved those stunts. The only downside was that there were quite a few accidents, and he saw some gruesome things occur. Air shows were dangerous as dare devil pilots and acrobats tried to outperform each other by flying higher, adding death defying spirals and upside-down flying antics. Even the wing walkers tried to give their scariest acts more excitement which sometimes ended in a fall with either a serious injury or death. But this did not deter his young adoration of airplanes.

In Calexico, there was a street with a whole row of tamarack trees. Bobby loved to go there and climb into the trees. The tamarack trees were very tall and held very fine, flexible needles. While he climbed the trees, he would pull the needles off and suck on them until he pulled the saltiness out. One day, Bobby hauled some planks up into the tree and built a platform. In his mind's eye, he believed it looked like an airplane. Bobby would lie down on the planks and gaze up into the sky. With the wind whooshing though the branches, swishing the needles back and forth, he believed he was flying in an airplane. Tree flying led Bobby to develop his passion for aviation.

Chapter 3

For me, sitting still is harder than any kind of work.

Annie Oakley

The Great Depression impacted the lives of everyone in Raul and Jessie's household. Unemployment was high in Southern California, and many migrant camps popped up in the fields from Calexico to San Diego, making it harder and harder for the locals to make ends meet. About this time, Raul and Jessie chose to send Bobby to live with Jessie's mother, Eva Shelton Wolf, in Oklahoma. During this time in his life Bobby developed his love for country and the cowboy lifestyle. Eva Wolf Shelton and her companion, Tom, worked at the celebrated 101 Ranch in Oklahoma. Eva was the ranch cook, and Tom was the foreman.

The Miller Brothers 101 Ranch was a growing entrainment venue borne out of the rodeo circuit of the old west. At the time, it was as popular as the budding Ringling Bros. and Barnum & Bailey Circus and Hollywood's vaudeville shows. The ranch's shows traveled the nation and were featured in Europe. It grew in popularity due to both its Hollywood connections and its renowned Wild West shows featuring Buffalo Bill, Wild Bill Cody, Annie Oakley, Will Rogers, and the notorious Apache, Geronimo.

Bobby traveled to the 101 Ranch by train. He really didn't know what to expect. Though he knew his grandmother well, he did not know the man she lived with on the ranch. Bobby knew even less about the 101 Ranch, and he didn't really understand why his parents sent him away. On the train to the ranch, he read what he could in the headlines of newspapers lying on the benches. He was intrigued by the famous names of cowboys he read about as he had seen some names in the magazines he delivered. The 101 Ranch seemed to be well known, and he glimpsed a few people on the train who looked like the Hollywood-type trick riders or cowgirls with their fancy western clothing.

Jessie made some meals for Bobby for the train ride, but they could not afford a sleeper car, so he sat quietly in his seat through the night, dozing off now and then. His one piece of luggage leaned up against his seat. There were other children on the train. One boy about his age was traveling with a little sister. The boy told him they had been sent to a farm to work since their parents couldn't feed them anymore. He guessed that was true for him too, but he didn't know if he was going to have to work for his living. When he arrived in Ponca City, Eva was waiting on the platform. Eva took his hand and led him to a horse-drawn wagon where they climbed into the back. The wagon bumped its way down the dusty road.

When he arrived at the ranch, he was amazed at the wide entrance gate, the big grand house, and the number of buildings that made up the ranch. There were many people walking around; it was a busy place. He saw a corral, several small barns, a huge silo, and a big show barn. There were animals and lots of horses. Eva pointed out where the ranch hands slept, a building for the cowboys, and where the cowgirls stayed. As they walked past the corral and big barn, she stopped at a small cabin set back in the woods. She opened the door and said this was their home. There was a living room with a stone fireplace, a kitchen off to one side, and a wooden table for eating. He saw a door to a bedroom off the kitchen. Eva pointed to the ladder and said his sleeping area was in the loft. The washroom was out the back door behind the kitchen.

Eva had a quiet smile. She was thin and wore wire glasses. Her hair was curly but not stylish the way the cowgirls wore their hair. She wore a skirt and button-up top with frills around the collar. Bobby felt her hands and thought they were rough when she touched his cheek. She gave him a big hug, and her arms were strong. Bobby thought she worked hard as the cook, feeding all these people, and she must get tired. She told him to put his things away and meet her outside.

Bobby climbed up the ladder and found a small bed with an Indian blanket, a washbowl, and an old mirror on the wall. A chair stood beside the bed. He took a moment and washed his face and combed his hair the way his mother told him to do. He climbed back down the ladder and wondered when he would meet Eva's boyfriend, Tom.

Eva was standing outside the door when he opened it, and Bobby saw some trucks hauling horses pull into the ranch driveway. Some of the men began to gather near the corral, and one of the men waved to Eva. He was tall and wore a brown cowboy hat. Eva told Bobby to go over to the man as she turned to walk toward the cook house. Bobby started toward the man.

As he drew close, the man said, "I'm Tom, Bobby. I have a job for you. These trucks have some new horses for the ranch. I want you to sit on the fence right here and watch each of the horses as they come off the truck. I want you to look for one that has a twinkle in its eye, that looks intelligent, and has character." He turned and looked right at Bobby. "Can you do that?" he asked.

Bobby didn't say anything, but he shook his head up and down and climbed up to sit on the fence and watch. Tom walked away to help unload the horses. One by one, the horses were led off the three trucks, taken to the corral, inspected, and then led into the big barn. As they unloaded the last trailer, a black-and-white palomino was led off the truck. It was a little scraggly looking and wasn't as big as the other horses. The horse turned its head and looked right at Bobby. Bobby felt an instant connection and looked to see if there was a twinkle in its eyes, and he thought for sure the horse smiled at him. He jumped down off the fence and followed the ranch hand leading him into the barn. One of the cowboys stopped him and told him he couldn't go in the barn and shut the door, so Bobby ran around the corner and climbed up on a water barrel to look in the window.

The black-and-white palomino held his head down low as the ranch hand led him into a stall. Bobby thought he looked sad. Maybe he was taken away from his parents and this was the first time he was in a new place all alone too. He hoped that because it was small, the black-and-white palomino would be used by the pretty cowgirls and not by some of the men who looked like they were rough with the horses. He heard Eva call his name, so he jumped off the barrel and headed back to the cabin to see her and Tom standing in the doorway of the cabin. He realized that Tom was the man his grandmother lived with in the cabin. The three of them sat around the dinner table, and Eva asked Tom about the horses. Tom began to talk about the quality of the horses, how some were for trick riding, some were for the show, a new horse for Bill Cody, and one for the clown act. As he talked about the horses and some of the men who would be riding them, Bobby was fascinated and tried to stay awake. It wasn't long before he laid his head on the table and fell fast asleep.

The next morning, he woke up hearing Tom call him to the living room. "Bobby," he said, "every morning at 7:00 a.m., I want you to meet me right here at the bottom of the ladder. You are a good-sized boy and healthy. There are chores that you are responsible for every day. All of us on the ranch work for their keep, and that includes you too. Eva has some breakfast for you, and then I'll show you your chores."

Eva handed Bobby a sack with an egg sandwich and an apple. He took it and followed Tom out the door and down to the barn. He pointed out the corral to Bobby and said that he could sit on the fence but never go into the corrals. The ranch hands and the cowboys used the corrals for training, and he could get hurt if he got in the way. The doors to the big barn were open, and he showed Bobby how the horses were lined up in the stalls. A ranch hand walked up to them, and Tom told Bobby to stay with the man.

The man showed Bobby how to put a moral on the horses for feeding and how to care for the horses by putting fresh hay and water in their stalls when they were out for training. He even learned how to muck the stalls. It was a lot of work, and once he figured out how to keep his hands from being nipped by the horses' teeth, he was able to put the feed bags on right. Mucking the stalls was dirty work, but he liked doing a good job.

The best part of the day was when he was able to feed the black-and-white palomino. He would sit back on the hay and eat his lunch and watch it. Bobby thought the horse was beautiful. Even though he had never ridden a horse, he hoped someday he would be allowed to ride him. He learned that the black-and-white palomino was for the circus acts. The cowboy clown manager was a nice guy, and he treated the black-and-white palomino well. Sometimes Bobby would sneak sugar cubes or carrots off the counter when Eva wasn't looking and hide them in his pocket to give to it to the palomino while he was working in the barn. He would stand inside the show tent when they rehearsed the clown acts and watch the black-and-white palomino. The palomino was a good horse, and Bobby dreamed that he would own it one day.

One afternoon, the clown manager asked Bobby if he wanted to groom the black-and-white palomino. Bobby was overjoyed, and the clown manager showed him how to comb the horse's hair and clean the hooves after he came back in from training. Tom came to watch him one day, and the clown manager stood next to him. As they shared a cigarette together, they laughed, and Bobby saw the clown manager point at Bobby. He thought he may have done something wrong. Tom looked at him straight in the eye, but Tom didn't smile.

A few mornings later when he climbed down the ladder, Tom wasn't there, and Eva was standing in the kitchen alone. She said Tom wanted to talk to him and he should have a seat at the table. Bobby sat and thought that he was in for big trouble. He thought back to time when he saw Tom looking at him when he was talking to the clown manager. When his dad would give him a talking to, it was never good. Tom walked in the door and sat at the table next to him.

"Bobby," he said with a serious expression on his face, "the men think you are old enough to start exercising the black-and-white palomino. I know you have never ridden a horse, but I think it's time you learn. Do you think you are ready?"

Bobby tried hard not to smile but to be businesslike, so he nodded his head. Tom handed him some cowboy boots, and Eva handed him a present wrapped in brown paper. "Go ahead, Bobby, open your gift." It was pair of chaps! Eva said she made them herself. That day, Tom took Bobby out to learn to ride. It wasn't easy, and it took Bobby a while to catch on. He wore his new boots and chaps every day, and he began to exercise the black-and-white palomino as a part of his daily chores.

That same evening as he got ready for bed, he thought of Raul and Jessie. Sometimes he really missed his mom and dad. He missed his brothers and sisters. Lots of times he thought if they could only see him now. He knew he was not just a boy anymore and he had grown up a lot. At the ranch, it was busy, and he enjoyed hearing the cowboys singing around the camp-fire at night. Eva was a good cook, and he never doubt-ed she loved him. Tom was a good foreman of the ranch, and he was good to Bobby too. He liked hearing about the tales of the cowboy and cow-girl antics, like Geronimo shooting bison from the front seat of a car, that Tom would talk about at the dinner table. The three shared many laughs.

Chapter 4

Don't let yesterday use up too much of today.

Will Rogers

One morning, Tom gave Bobby a rifle. It wasn't big or fancy, but it was good for shooting mice and jackrabbits in the desert. It was a Sunday, so Bobby didn't have too many chores when he went out into the desert. He knew some of the hands practiced shooting in a clearing. He was going to try to see if his aim was good. He set some cans and bottles on the stands and stood back to try a shot when he heard some rustling in the brush behind him. He turned, and there stood an old Indian who looked at him and shook his head. All the Indian said was "Humph," and he shook his head at Bobby. The old Indian walked over and took the rifle from Bobby and pointed to the sight, showing him how to stand with his legs spread a little a part and brace the rifle with his shoulder. He aimed and fired, knocking the first bottle right off the stand. He reloaded and handed the rifle back to Bobby.

Footsteps came up the path, and Tom walked into the clearing. "Geronimo, the Millers are looking for you. You'd best get back." Geronimo, the notorious Apache Indian and member of the Miller's Wild West

Show, was standoffish, and this was the first time Bobby met him face-to-face. Though there were many famous characters, cowboys, and cowgirls on the ranch like Will Rogers, Buck Jones, and Annie Oakley, Bobby stayed close to his home and observed them from afar. As Geronimo walked away Tom turned to look at Bobby and spent the rest of the afternoon teaching him how to use the rifle. He told him not to get too attached to it because he didn't know how much longer Bobby would be with them.

That evening Eva sat at the dinner table listening to Tom talk about their day. Tom, she mused, was not her husband. It was not that he didn't want to be, but she was done with marriage. Her first husband, George Washington Shelton, died in the Civil War. He was young, the father of her two children, and he wanted to please his brothers and sisters by taking up their fight. She and George hadn't seen eye to eye on this, and he went south to fight anyway and left her and the kids in Ohio. After he died, she took up with Hank. He was such a looker and had a way with the women. He talked of city lights and money out west—a new way of living, he said. Eva had been caught up in his stories and dreams, and he persuaded her to put away her kids for a while as she followed him from town to town. Eventually she saw that it was all smoke and lies. She may have been married to Hank, but it was not a happy marriage, and he finally ran off with a Hollywood girl. It was for the best because his lifestyle was wearing her down and she wanted her children back. She considered her judgment of men to be poor and not to be trusted.

Then there was Tom. He came to her rescue. He was as honest as they came, and she knew he would never leave her side. Of the few places they lived, he always craved the "Wild West." He was a gentleman cowboy at heart. He loved the ranch, and he loved the men and women he worked with. And he loved Bobby. Eva knew they were past having children, and their companionship is what mattered the most. She would not have it any other way. She trusted Tom. They were happy despite whatever they faced.

"Tom," Eva started. "I received a letter from Jessie today." Both man and boy stopped eating and looked up at her. How she hated telling them what the letter said. She hesitated. Tom always told her it was best to spit it out, that it was no use holding back uncomfortable news. "Raul and Jessie want Bobby to come back." She saw the clouds in Bobby's eyes as he went from joy to sadness within a split second. Tom looked at her, and his look spoke a hundred different emotions.

Tom began to eat again, and then setting his fork down, he said, "I hear rumors that the ranch is not doing well. If we move out to California, the Millers can give my job to someone who needs it more than me." Bobby was quiet and holding his breath. His feelings were mixed. If he left, he would leave the black-and-white palomino, the ranch, and all the people he knew now; they felt like family to him. On the other hand, he would see his mom and dad and his brothers and sisters and be home—his real home.

Tom stood up from the table. "Best we plan, Eva. We'll take Bobby back to his parents together. We'll find a new place to live and work." He covered her hand with his for moment. Then he walked out the door.

Eva looked at Bobby and said, "I'll write your mother and let her know to expect us next month." Bobby smiled at Eva, but it was a bittersweet smile as he climbed his ladder to the loft. This was a good time with Eva and Tom. He didn't know what to expect when he got back to California and saw his parents, but at least his grandmother and Tom were coming.

On the day of their departure, several of the ranch hands and cowboys came to see them off. They loaded one of the ranch's wagons with their belongings, and everyone started saying their goodbyes. One of the cowboys walked over and shook Bobby's hand. Bobby knew him as the singing cowboy. He had read about him in some of the Western magazines.

"Bobby, you took good care of my horse. We will miss you," the man said.

"Thank you, Mr. Rogers," Bobby said as he climbed into the wagon.

The train ride to California was long, but this time Bobby was able to enjoy the sleeper car with Tom and Eva.

Once back in California, it wasn't long before Eva and Tom found a job as caretakers at a ranch over the border in Mexico not too far from the town of El Centro where Raul moved the family. Bobby continued to visit his grandparents from time to time and do chores around their new ranch.

Settling back into life in California, Bobby discovered the new town of El Centro. His father worked for the theater company in the town, and his mother found odd jobs to help make ends meet while she cared for the children. The family was still poor, and the Depression continued to affect their way of life.

By the time Bobby was eleven, Hollywood was booming. Everyone wanted to live in California. Going to the movies was the grandest thing to do. Bobby still liked to enter the contests at the movie theater, as did Jessie, even though Raul wasn't happy about it. Jessie would go often and win. She felt she was doing her part while being close to Raul and the kids. Raul did not understand, and their quarrels came more often.

During these later years of the Depression before World War II, the dust bowl settled into the Midwest. The rise of Hitler began in Germany as the United States continued to fight poverty. The demands of farmers and workers as they trekked westward to start their lives over again in California brought increased political pressure. Bobby heard about the dust bowl and often thought about how this affected the people he met in Oklahoma. Some of those men and women moved to California during this time and were famous on the screen, people like Will Rogers and Tex Ritter.

The United States was hit by terrible storms during this period. After the Homestead Act of 1862, thousands of settlers moved to the Midwest, and over the years, trees were cut down and acreage across the prairies was plowed and left bare. When the storms hit, there was nothing but dusty, dry land. The wind whipped so hard that an area would be dark for days and farms and towns would be covered with dust. Many farmers had to flee their farms because their crops were wiped out. In Texas and Oklahoma, the dust was so bad the birds would not fly. The families that left soon became migrant workers alongside the Mexican workers in California. Many of these families moved to the Imperial Valley where Bobby lived. There were nineteen states affected by the dust storms. These conditions and changes made an impact on the culture of that time and was captured in the book *The Grapes of Wrath*, written by John Steinbeck in 1939 when Bobby was sixteen years old. This was the same year the Miller Brothers 101 Ranch in Oklahoma closed its doors.

Chapter 5

*Courage is being scared to death
and saddling up anyway.*

John Wayne

The year 1936 brought storm clouds to Europe. Hitler became Germany's president and children in Europe started learning about guns. Increasingly, European children attended military schools instead of traditional schools. The German Volkswagen Beetle made its debut. Hitler wanted to be like Henry Ford and began mass-producing the Beetle.

Labor unions grew in the United States, becoming very strong and frequently holding strikes. Talk in Bobby's home centered more and more on labor strikes and the looming war. Raul become active in the labor union movement. General Motors shut down once because of the strikes. These strikes affected Raul in a way that Bobby did not understand. Sometimes people would come over to the house in the evenings and talk about "the Reds." Bobby learned that Reds were people who were involved in some type of working-class struggle. Although Bobby never really knew exactly who they were or where they came from, he could hear the heated conversations in his home.

Raul said the Reds were going to camp outside the town and stir up trouble. Bobby listened as his dad cautioned him to stay away from them. He saw that people would come into town with all their goods strapped on their cars looking for work. Neighbors in town started putting up signs telling the Reds to go away. Raul and the men who came to see him would leave the house late at night and return in the morning. Bobby believed his dad went with a group of men to run the Reds out of town. Raul justified his actions by saying jobs were scarce enough for the men of El Centro without outsiders trying to take away their jobs. Raul's actions created more quarrels, and Jessie and Bobby's home life became tense. Jessie did not disguise the fact that she was thoroughly against whatever Raul was doing. Raul argued back that it was part of the labor union movement to drive the Reds out. Bobby did not think that was true, but he really didn't know.

Bobby learned that during the time he spent on the 101 Ranch, the family lived in several houses before settling down in the house in El Centro. Home life suffered, and his parents' relationship was often intense.

Eva and Tom visited often, and many times Bobby was able to visit them. Visiting them was a highlight in his life during this time. The first ranch house Eva and Tom lived in was a tiny house. The house had canvas windows instead of glass windows. One day when visiting Eva, Bobby watched as she was sitting by the dresser curling her hair. He saw Eva using things that looked like pliers in her hair. She had two of them, and they were stuck in a kerosene lantern. They didn't yet have electricity, so she stuck them in the lamp until they were hot, and then she put them in her hair and rolled her hair up.

All around Eva's living area were dime western novels. She and Tom loved reading them! The novels were larger than the magazines Bobby used to sell, about 8 × 10. Tom brought his cowboy gear from the 101 Ranch and often reminisced about the cowboys' antics. Bobby would listen to the stories repeatedly; the stories never got old, and he often longed for his time on the ranch. Tom and Eva both smoked Bull Durham cigarettes. The tobacco came in a little white pouch. In the front of the pouch were little papers, like tissues, about two and a half inches long. Tom would make cigarettes out of the papers. Bobby was fascinated watching him roll them because Tom could do it all with one hand! He would pull the tissue out, dump the tobacco in, roll, and lick it. Bobby didn't remember ever seeing his grandmother do it, but he knew they both smoked the same cigarettes.

Radios were in their infancy in the 1930s. Some of the boys Bobby knew liked to make ham radios. Ham radios were a new means of communication used by landline telegraphers who had to leave their jobs to go out to work on a ship or a government station. It wasn't long before ham radios caught on and people started building their own.

One of Bobby's friends had a little shack behind his house where they kept radio equipment. The two of them would experiment with tubes and wires and eventually were able build radios so they would talk to people around the world. Raul opened an electronic shop in his garage to earn extra income, and Bobby spent hours learning how to make things work using tubes and wire. His friends would ask him to bring supplies for them, which he did from time to time. He knew never to ask Raul, but he managed to scrounge around and find wire and other supplies to trade. His best friend's mother made wonderful biscuits and would sell them around town. Bobby would take his wire and tubes over to his friend's house, and his mother would trade him for a tray of twelve biscuits! Bobby felt those were the best trades he ever made!

Commercial operators were not happy with homemade radios because their commercial radios would get jammed. They started calling these amateur operators "hams" to make them mad, but the name caught on. Though Bobby was interested in ham radios, he preferred building model airplanes. It was about this time that Jessie and Raul divorced. Rumors were that Jessie met someone in town and had an affair. Bobby and the children were never told about what happened, but their father told them the church granted him the divorce, and the children were not allowed to see their mother until they were eighteen.

Chapter 6

Bite off more than you can chew, then chew it.

Ella Williams

When Raul and Jessie divorced, and Jessie left the household, Bobby and Lucille assumed the household chores. As the two oldest of eight children, they had no choice but to step up to the plate. Lucille handled much of the daily care of her younger siblings. In fact, she was forced to quit school for a while because there was no one to look after the youngest sister who was not yet school age. Lucille was unhappy about this. She enjoyed her friends and did not want to stay home with a child all day. Bobby continued with school and now had paper routes each morning. He added cooking and cleaning to his mornings and nights. He was not pleased with his new situation any more than Lucille. Raul was not the type of father who discussed issues with his children. His word was law, and no one questioned him. If Raul suspected Bobby and Lucille were not on board with the changes in their lives, he never spoke to them about it.

Raul was working all the time, and Bobby was given control of the family when his father was at work. One Saturday, Bobby was told to wash his father's car while his father was at work. Even though Raul had grown stern and silent, he still loved his cars and had a new Chevy. Bobby's younger brothers, Wayne and George, begged Bobby to let them help wash the car.

Bobby quickly put Wayne on the side of the car and George on the front. The brothers worked well together and put their hearts into giving the car a good scrub.

"Hey, Bobby, check out the rear. We can't get to the underside." Wayne showed Bobby some dirt caked on the underside. Bobby eyed the car and decided he needed to move the car up a little so he could reach the back better. He climbed in and started the motor. The car suddenly lurched forward, pinning George up against the front of the house.

"He's dead! His bones are crushed!" shouted Wayne. "Bobby! You crushed him to pieces!"

Bobby, white-faced and shaking, ran to the front where he found George bent over in laughter. George was a tough kid and withstood numerous calamities in his short life, and the three boys made a pact to never tell their father about the incident.

After lunch, Bobby started to clean the inside of the car and rinse off the motor. Finishing his task, he went around to start the car to drive it back to where his father had left it. The car would not start! Bobby became frantic because the afternoon was getting on, and it wouldn't be too long before his father returned home. Bobby knew that spark plugs were a key to starting the engine. He had seen his father change them so he thought the answer might lie in the plugs Pulling all the wires out of the car, Bobby grabbed his bike and sped to see his father's friend Gus at the gas station. Gus, working under the hood of an old Ford, listened to Bobby's frantic explanation of the problem.

"Bobby, the wires are wet. You need to dry them, son, before you put them back in. Go inside and get a rag and dry them good," he hollered over the hum of the Ford engine. Gus never looked up.

Bobby dried the wires and raced back to put them back in the engine. Once they were hooked back in the car, he tried to start the car. It still wouldn't work! Jumping back on his bicycle and heading back to Gus's station, all Bobby could think of was how he had ruined his father's car.

Standing with his hands on his wide hips, Gus watched Bobby coming up the road in a flurry of dust.

"Gus! I dried them and put them back and the car still won't start! What can I do?"

"Well," chuckled Gus slowly, wiping his oily hands on the deep pockets of his overalls, "did you put them back in the right order?" Gus could tell by Bobby's face that he hadn't.

"Come inside, and I will draw you a picture," said Gus, walking toward the old wooden station door.

Gus drew Bobby a picture with the wires labeled and numbered. Bobby pedaled back home and worked on the car for two more hours before he could get the car to start. Bobby's father arrived home from work minutes after Bobby had placed the keys back on the hook by the front door. No one ever mentioned a word to Raul about the events of the day.

Around this time, Bobby began working for the newspaper in the evening after his father got home from work. Bobby kept his morning route, but Sam, the local distributor, offered him a new job. Sam, who always looked rumpled like he slept in his clothes, would take Bobby with him each evening to San Diego where they would pick up the newspaper bundles and bring them back to El Centro to distribute at corner drugstores. This task was accomplished in the middle of the night. Bobby just had time to finish his chores and homework and fix dinner before heading out to his new job.

One evening when Sam and Bobby had picked up the newspapers in San Diego, they were driving through the mountains when it became very foggy. The steep drop to the desert floor was a dangerous drive. Sam picked up a rolled newspaper and started hitting himself on the head.

"Hey, what are you doing? The fog is crazy, and we can't see!" Bobby yelled.

Sam screeched, "You see what I am doing? Every time you see me getting sleepy, you need to start hitting me on the top of the head with a paper. These are narrow two-lane roads, and I can NOT fall asleep! If I do, we will plunge right off the cliff!"

There were many following nights when Bobby had to hit Sam over the head. Sam never complained and would reward Bobby with a big tip on those nights. On another one of the trips across the mountains, the fog rolled in so heavy and thick Sam and Bobby could barely see the front of their truck. Sam gave Bobby a flashlight and told him to get out and sit on the front fender.

"Now, you shine that light where I need to drive, Bobby. I cannot see a thing, and you know how the sides are so steep they drop off to nothing," said Gus. By this time, Bobby was used to Gus coming up with some strange requests, but this seemed the craziest yet—and the scariest. On the other hand, Bobby knew that Gus was right, and he didn't want to topple over the sides of the mountains either.

Bobby climbed out on the big fender in the dark. He spent two long, agonizing hours shining the flashlight back to the road too many times. When they arrived home, the big tip Gus gave Bobby did not make up for the fact that he was exhausted.

It wasn't long after that incident that Raul made Bobby quit the job. He could see how drained Bobby was all the time, and even though the pay was good, Raul said it was too much work and it would affect his schoolwork. Raul needed Bobby's paychecks so instead of the ride over the mountains, Raul found him work after school with an electrical company.

Seemingly out of the blue, Raul decided to bring his stepfather, Pedro, to live with them. Bobby had never met his grandfather before. There were times when he was younger that his mother would go up to San Francisco and take Bobby along. On these occasions, they would visit Raul's mother, Sophie, and her sister Mary. Bobby knew there was a grandfather somewhere but guessed he didn't live with his grandmother. He heard his grandmother say that Pedro lived in Tucson, Arizona.

So, one day, Pedro showed up with a tattered suitcase and told the children he was going to live with them and take care of them. Bobby never developed a relationship with Pedro. There was an aloofness he felt around him. They did not outwardly dislike each other, but they never really got along. Pedro assumed most of the cooking, but Bobby and Lucille still did all the work around the house and washed the clothes while Pedro supervised. Life for Bobby settled into a new pattern with Pedro in the background smoking his pipe.

Now that Pedro was in the household, Bobby was free to get involved in high school sports. Bobby's first choice was playing tennis, and he enjoyed the game, the competition, and the praise that Coach Maxwell sent his way. One day after practice, Bobby walked over to the boys who were practicing football and joined in their game of running, throwing, and tackling each other. The football coach, watching from the sidelines, approached Bobby after practice.

"Hey, Bobby, why aren't you playing on the football team? You have some skill," the coach said. When Bobby explained that he was playing tennis, the coach told Bobby that he would fix it with Coach Maxwell. Although Coach Maxwell was not happy with the situation, he released Bobby from tennis. Bobby's football career was short-lived. One night when he was playing center and was handed the ball, he ran toward the wrong goal and was tackled by his own team member.

Bobby then decided it was time to try track. He was a fast runner and ran for the team until he was injured. A fellow team member tripped over Bobby in a baton relay, and the boy's spikes ripped down Bobby's heel, which ended his running career.

During Bobby's high school years, things were changing quickly in the world. Bobby would read the headlines on his paper route. The headlines were always about Hitler and how he was trying to take over the world. Hitler's armies invaded Poland, and everyone knew a war was coming. Bobby watched some of his older friends enlist in the military. He envied those boys and wondered if some day he would be asked to enlist. He knew he was too young now but hoped he could join the military if a war started. Being the eldest, he was not sure

One night, Raul told Bobby he wanted to have a talk with him after dinner. This was rare because Raul did not usually talk with his children in the evenings. After Jessie left, Raul became reclusive and ruled with orders instead of embracing a home life with his children. Occasionally, Raul would sit with the oldest boys and talk, but mostly they would all sit and listen to the radio. Bobby naturally was a little wary about having a serious conversation with his father and could not imagine what it was going to be about.

Raul told Bobby that very soon the United States was going to be involved in a war and Bobby would be expected to enroll in the military. He told Bobby he didn't want him to enter the army but rather join the Coast Guard. When the time was right, he would send Bobby to live with his grandmother, Sophie, who was now living in San Francisco. Raul told him that when he arrived in San Francisco, he was to immediately enroll in the Coast Guard. Bobby was only sixteen when he had this conversation with his father, and it was never spoken about again until sometime near his seventeenth birthday.

Chapter 7

Life is like riding a bicycle.
To keep your balance, you must keep moving forward.

Albert Einstein

In the middle of Bobby's junior year of high school, 1939, the war in Europe raged forward. France and England declared war on Germany. In the United States, many people sensed that a war was imminent; however, daily life continued as if it could not possibly impact them.

In high school, Bobby found himself struggling with English history. He did not like the subject very much, and he had a difficult time keeping up with the course. Usually, Bobby was a good student and took his studies seriously. Work was taking a toll on him, and he wondered if this was part of the problem. One day, his teacher, an elderly soft-spoken woman, asked Bobby to remain after class. She sat Bobby down and talked to him a long time that afternoon. Bobby was discouraged listening to her and felt like he was failing. The teacher told Bobby he was wasting his time in her class and would be better off changing classes.

Bobby was bewildered because he didn't know what he should do. The teacher explained that he should be taking something that he enjoyed and suggested he try the print shop. Bobby wasn't quite sure if this was something he wanted to do, but he quietly followed his teacher over to the shop to talk with the instructor. Arrangements were made, and Bobby joined the print shop. It was an actual shop where the students worked on machines, electric motors, and welding. To Bobby's amazement, this was right up his alley, and he thrived in the environment.

Bobby learned to use the presses to print materials for the high school. He learned he had a knack for machinery. Bobby and a classmate were asked to print tickets for an upcoming carnival the school was holding. Bobby and his friend decided to print $100 worth of extra tickets so they could use them free at the fair. The teachers running the fair must have come up $100 short when they counted their money, but Bobby and his friend were never caught, and they never confessed. Although Bobby enjoyed his free rides at the carnival, he felt ashamed of what he did. He wondered if he was heading down that wrong path that everyone was always talking about.

Soon afterward, President Roosevelt was elected for a third term, and discussion about enforcing the Selective Service Act was in the news. Just as Raul predicted, if the United States entered the war within a month, the draft lottery would begin. All men between the ages of twenty-one and thirty-five were required to sign up for the draft. Bobby, only sixteen, was still working his morning paper routes and not really worried about the draft. He knew his father had already made plans for him. With the threat of war increasing daily, Bobby wondered when his father would tell him to go to San Francisco and join the Coast Guard. Raul remained silent on the subject for a while.

It was a hot day in July when Raul told Bobby it was time to go to San Francisco to stay with his grandmother. He was 16 years old. Bobby was both subdued and excited. He knew his life was getting ready to change drastically, but he could not see or imagine what it would be like. For as long as he could remember, his life had been even keeled. His days were filled with taking care of his siblings and himself while working and going to school. School suddenly crossed his mind. He would not be able to finish high school. He was sad thinking about it but knew many kids who did not finish. He realized that some had to leave to go to work full time to support family, and many said they were getting ready to go fight the upcoming war. The excitement that Bobby was feeling overrode his feelings of high school.

Raul told Bobby that Garo, a man living at his grandmother's house, would come to get him in El Centro. Bobby wondered what he should pack to begin his new life, so he actually packed very little in a small bag. When Garo arrived, they took the train to Los Angeles and then transferred to a train heading to San Francisco. Bobby was so excited to arrive in his grandmother's city. As he walked up the steep steps to her house, he was still thinking about his future. He realized along the trip that he was looking forward to everything life had to offer him.

When Bobby entered Sophie's house, she greeted him warmly. "I am so glad you are here, Bobby. We will have a wonderful time before you have to leave for the Coast Guard. It will be nice for me to have you all to myself for a while," she said. She pulled him in for a tight bear hug.

Sophie was a tall, heavy woman with a wide, beautiful smile. Her dark hair was peppered with streaks of white, and there was an aura of strength and dignity about her. Bobby could easily see she must have been quite pretty when she was younger. Her features reminded him of the Indians he met in Oklahoma, and her dark eyes and skin color were like the pictures of the goddesses of Greek mythology. He could not picture his grandmother and Pedro together.

Sophie told Bobby that Garo's son had moved up the street and opened a little print shop and was no longer living with them so Bobby could have his room. Sophie led Bobby down a narrow hall and told him he could come to dinner when he finished putting his things away. Bobby quickly put his few things away in the dresser drawers in the small room and went in search of his grandmother.

Bobby spent his first couple of days working around the house and doing small, odd jobs for his grandmother. Sophie had a large shed out back of the house and raised geraniums that she sold to people in town. Bobby loved the smell of the flowers and quickly learned how to transplant them and start new plants. He cherished this time with his grandmother. He felt so peaceful and at ease sitting beside Sophie while working with the small plants. There were no responsibilities pulling at him go to work, to feed the children, or to deliver papers.

It was truly a stress-free time for him. Bobby made friends with the boys who lived next door. They had a car and would take Bobby with them into town to see a movie or just hang out. Sometimes Bobby would go over to his Aunt Mary's house and visit her. She was a hefty woman and loved to cook. She looked a lot like Sophie but younger. She rented out her rooms to lodgers. Every time she saw Bobby, she would laugh and say he was just too skinny! Then she would rush to fix him something to eat.

Bobby enjoyed this peaceful lifestyle for a few weeks until Pedro moved to San Francisco. Pedro found a job in a body shop and came over to tell Bobby it was time for him to go to work. He took Bobby to the body shop and put him to work. Even though Bobby did not feel close to Pedro and their relationship was strained, Bobby enjoyed his time there. The owner of the shop had an old car engine that he was working on and encouraged Bobby to repair it. The shop owner taught Bobby how to change cylinders and work on cars. He truly felt home working with the machinery. The best part was Bobby was given a Model A Coupe to drive back and forth to work.

Several weeks after Bobby had started working at the auto shop, he received a letter from his father asking how he was doing getting into the Coast Guard. Bobby hadn't really done anything toward signing up for the Coast Guard because he loved his new life.

One morning, Pedro came to the house and said he was there to take Bobby to sign up for the Coast Guard. Pedro walked down the street toward the courthouse hall and pointed to where Bobby was to go. Then Pedro turned around and walked away. Bobby walked into the hall and saw a large official man in a uniform sitting behind the front desk. Bobby walked up to him and told him he was there to sign up for the Coast Guard. The man in the uniform told him he was in the right place and to sit down. He asked Bobby a lot of questions, and Bobby filled out a lot of papers. Bobby was not yet seventeen, and he was told he could not join until he was seventeen, and even then, he had to have a certificate signed by both parents giving him permission to enter the military because he was still a minor.

There was also an issue with Bobby's teeth. Being that a dentist was not a priority in El Centro, Bobby needed to have several cavities filled before the military would accept him. Finally, he headed home with papers in tow and explained everything to Sophie. His birthday was just around the corner, and as soon as Bobby turned seventeen, Raul and Sophie arranged for a dentist to fill his teeth. Somehow Sophie found Jessie, and she signed the papers. It had been over two years since Bobby had seen his mother, and he did not even know where she lived. He didn't ask since he was not yet old enough to visit in person with his mother. According to the divorce agreement, Bobby and his siblings were not allowed to see their mother until they were 18 years of age.

A month or two after his seventeenth birthday, he took all the paperwork back to the man in the military office. The officer told Bobby that he would receive his papers and assignment in the mail. Several more months passed, and Bobby finally received a letter in the mail with orders to report to the San Diego Naval Training School in September 1940.

Chapter 8

Always be a first-rate version of yourself
instead of a second-rate version of someone else.

Judy Garland

In 1940, the movie *The Grapes of Wrath* came out to the theaters. Even though the years of the dust bowl and the Great Depression were ending, this movie was a true depiction of what was happening in the midwestern parts of the United States. In the same year, nylon stockings became wildly popular. The material had been presented at the World's Fair in New York the previous year. Millions of nylon stockings were sold instantly. Women loved them!

Bobby received his orders and was to report at 7:00 a.m. at the Union Square train station in Los Angeles. He took the train from San Francisco and waited at the Union Square train station for someone from the military to meet him. Bobby did not know what to expect and decided to just do what he was told. He carried a few personal items with him. He joined up with a group of about twenty or thirty other enlistees that were mostly around his age. Once the military escorts arrived, he and the group of guys were hustled onto several navy buses that took them to the training station in San Diego. It was a long ride from Los Angeles.

The first stop for Bobby was to complete his physical. To his amazement, he weighed only ninety-three pounds! He was given several shots and then marched down the hall to a room with clothing and shoes. He received a sea bag and a hammock with a little mattress in it. He was told to put all his clothes in the sea bag and then put the mattress in the center of the pack. Then the hammock went around the whole thing. He was instructed to carry that around with him all day! Then he was assigned a unit. His unit was 40-114. All of these happenings in one day were difficult!

As Bobby started his indoctrination into military life that first day, he began to feel terribly sick. That evening around five o'clock, he and the men in his unit were all lined up around the flagpole. There were several groups there, not just guys from his unit. He began to hear a humming noise that he thought was an airplane. He looked up and then leaned over to the guy beside him to ask what the noise was, and that was the last thing he remembered. He woke up several hours later in the sick bay. He had passed out! The medics told him it was a reaction to all the shots. He wasn't the only newcomer in the sick bay that day! The medics called it cat fever, and he had flulike symptoms that lasted for several more days. Bobby had not had many shots in his life other than the smallpox vaccine and a couple shots when he had scarlet fever as a child.

Military life was a new experience for Bobby. He learned about so many things he didn't know even existed.

The second meal he had at boot camp was on a Sunday. He sat with guys in his unit at a long broad table in the mess hall. Food was served cafeteria style, and the guys would go up to the front where the cooks were serving food and carry their plates back to the table. Bobby stared at his plate. It had some big round things that looked like croquettes in gravy. When he cut into one, some brown juice squirted out; he took a bite.

"Hey, y'all, do you know what this is?" Bobby asked as he skewered the blob on his fork and held it up.

"It's fried oysters, man. Haven't you ever eaten them before?" the guy beside him shouted.

What in the world? Bobby was shocked! He grabbed his stomach and ran for the door, throwing up in the grass. In his mind, he pictured a squirmy oyster and decided then and there he would always check before he ate anything. There were a lot of strange foods he had never eaten in his life! The guys were all laughing when he came back in to sit down.

Of the clothes issued on the first day, he received whites, shirts, undershirts, bell bottom jeans, shorts, socks, white hats, and a couple of towels. He learned once you received that first issue, you had to buy anything you ruined or lost. His pay was $21 a month! During the first days of training, he had his first haircut, which was free, but he was told he had to pay for cuts after the first one. He learned how to scrub his clothes by laying them out on big boards in the yard. He was given brushes to scrub them with saltwater soap, and then he had to rinse them under big faucets with rushing water. Next, he hung them up on the line. He slept in a hammock and found that it was quite comfortable.

His life fell into a new routine, one that he got used to quickly. In the mornings, he would have fifteen minutes from the time the bugle blew, and the lights came on to put his stuff away and store it by the rails along the walls. Then he ran to take a shower and then ran to make it to muster. Bobby enjoyed the new life, the organization, and the friends he made. He found he was good at following orders.

There were several weeks of assembling and disassembling machine guns, rifles, and pistols. Bobby remembered much of the skills Tom taught him on the 101 Ranch and was thankful that he wasn't a newbie to guns.

There was something nagging Bobby, though. When he was assigned to boot camp, he was placed in the T Unit. In this unit, the teachers were always talking about navy ships. This was confusing because Bobby signed up for the Coast Guard. One morning, he went up to the chief and asked him how he would select his Coast Guard ship. He told his chief that he signed up for the Coast Guard. The chief started laughing and told Bobby that he didn't sign up for the Coast Guard; he signed up for the navy! So, Bobby felt he got suckered that day in San Francisco! The navy chief was sitting at that desk and signed him up before Bobby found the Coast Guard.

Bobby sent a letter to his father and Sophie. He never got an answer back, so Bobby assumed they were glad he got into something.

Bobby's training continued as the weeks went by. He was given a gas mask and sent into little huts on base. The trainers set off tear gas, and he would have to put his mask on in the dark and then run out another door with his unit. Most of the guys came out crying, including Bobby, because they couldn't get the mask on tight enough. But they learned, passed the test, and moved on to something new.

Every day, once in the morning and once in the evening, Bobby and his unit went to the grinder (a big parking lot). There were several big navy bands there, and they played while the trainees marched. They marched in different formations and learned some fancy marching, or so Bobby thought. The bands played some great music. There is where Bobby felt he cemented his love of big band music.

Bobby learned how to tie knots and about all the evils of life. It was such an interesting time for Bobby. He really enjoyed growing into adulthood, and during this experience, he made friends who stayed close to him for many years.

After Bobby finished basic training, he was transferred to another unit on the same base. This was called the north unit. There he studied recognition classes. Recognition training involves learning all the different types of aircraft and how to distinguish between friendly and enemy planes. Naval history and lists of ships were also covered in training. Then each guy in the unit was given a short interview with an officer. Bobby was asked various questions like what kind of profession or rating he wanted for his future. Bobby really didn't know how to answer these questions. He knew he had a knack for machinery, and he liked aviation. When he was in basic training, he was an apprentice seaman. Now in the north unit, he was a second-class seaman.

Entertainment was nonexistent in boot camp. Bobby really wanted to see more of the town and wondered when he would be able to go off base. Finally, in the last week of T Unit, he was allowed to go into San Diego for liberty. He left together with four of his new friends for a night on the town. They went to the movies and Balboa Park and took a walk on the beach. It was one of his finest memories.

One day, he was given a slip of paper and asked to write down what he wanted to do in the navy. He was asked to write down two or three places he wanted to go. Bobby thought of Oklahoma, Mexico, and San Francisco. Both San Francisco and Oklahoma were nice places, but he was up in the air about what he wanted to do. A guy was telling some of the others in the unit that the best job was on a tugboat. He said there were about six people on a tugboat, and they really didn't go anywhere. They just ran up and down the coast. Bobby thought maybe he would stay close to home if he put in for a tugboat and then added a minesweeper and a destroyer to be adventurous.

About a week later, Bobby was hanging around the bulletin boards with his friends to see what assignments were given. Bobby was assigned to the USS *Tangier*. He learned later that the *Tangier* was a seaplane tender His responsibility was to support the seaplanes. Soon Bobby had his graduation ceremony and was on his way to San Francisco for his first real assignment as a seaman.

Chapter 9

The expert in anything was once a beginner.

Unknown

It was the second week of March 1941 when Bobby received orders for the USS *Tangier*. He was supposed to report to the receiving station, Treasure Island, in San Francisco in April. He had two weeks' delayed orders and that meant he had two weeks' leave. He finally was going home! His first stop was to his house to see his dad and his siblings.

That trip was the first time Bobby met Audrey. Raul remarried while Bobby was away, and Audrey stepped into the mother's role caring for the younger children and supervising the household. She was a character in her own right and could stand toe-to-toe with Raul. She was a co-conspirator during Prohibition helping her brother's bootlegging business, and her first job was as a Harvey Girl near a rail station in the Midwest. Harvey Girls were well known women on the frontier that served men meals in the dining rooms of rail stations across the Midwest. They were the first group of women to work outside the home for wages. She was also a Comstock! The Comstock reputation was derived after a family owning the largest silver mine in Nevada. The family was known for their grit and determination Audrey was divorced with a little girl named Sally. Bobby never really got to know her well, but it was good knowing that someone was at the house, even if his brothers and sisters were not happy about it.

Two weeks later, he reported to San Francisco. The receiving station at Treasure Island was a large navy facility where men would come in from ships and wait for their new orders and reassignment. At times, there could be up to fifty men waiting for news. Treasure Island was also a navy training site. There was a large group waiting for the USS *Tangier* when Bobby arrived. He was told that the Tangier was across the bay in Oakland at a large shipyard called Moore's Dry Dock. His ship was being converted from a merchant ship to a seaplane tender.

Bobby learned that a tender would go to advanced bases in the islands or in the Pacific and set out floating buoys where the seaplanes could hook up to them. The seaplane crew would stay on the tender while the mechanics worked on the seaplanes. Bobby expected it to be busy with a continuous rotation of different people coming and going. He was excited that he would be doing something he felt good at and enjoyed. Bobby observed that there were guys coming from all over the place. Some were just starting out, like him, and some had ten to fifteen years' experience.

While waiting in San Francisco, he was instructed to support all the squadrons that were assigned to the

USS *Tangier*. It was here that Bobby met his best friends. He dropped the boyish name and introduced himself as Bob. He met Chet, Whitey, and Joe, and they became lifelong friends. They were all seventeen years old when they met at Treasure Island.

Bob had time to reflect on his new role and environment. Of course, there were young men his age that went the wrong way, drank a lot, and got themselves in trouble. He told his friends that those guys had to learn things the hard way. But he felt his group of friends all had come together for purpose—to become the crew of the USS *Tangier*. They waited at Treasure Island for six months until their ship was ready.

Chet quickly became Bob's best friend. They frequently went on liberty together. Sometimes they would take the train to Los Angeles. Whitey also went sometimes, but he was assigned as a radioman, and Bobby was just a seaman. In the beginning, Whitey and the guys didn't hang out much because they were different ranks. Chet and Bob became close friends after they were on the ship.

Chet and Bob went everywhere together. They learned that there were not as many girls as there were guys, so they often went out together with one girl! In San Francisco, there was one girl, Mary, who they took to the movies together. The only thing they had to pay for were the tickets for the movie or theater, and it didn't cost very much. Bob and Chet would go to the Golden Gate Theater. They saw Alice Faye, Harry James, and other actors and actresses. Other times, Bob and Chet would go out to Cliff House and the amusement park. For twenty-five cents, they could ride the Ferris wheel. Streetcars were free, so they explored all that San Francisco had to offer without getting into trouble. Bob was getting tired of waiting for the ship to be ready. He heard rumors that there were problems with shipyard strikes that kept delaying the ship work.

Bob was not one to waste his time, so he began studying to become seaman first class. He had to learn knots, nautical terms, and weather systems. He knew that seaman first class would earn him three stripes and a little more money.

Mary introduced Bob to a Marine. His name was Sacha, and Bob thought it would be good to have a Marine on his side since they oversaw security on base. You never knew when someone might have some trouble. Bob began to visit Sacha when off duty, and they soon became good friends. They often talked about their homes and what they wanted to do in the future.

One evening, Bob was sitting on Sacha's cot while Sacha was cleaning his .45 pistol. "Hey, Bob, take a look at it. What do you think? You have all that experience on the ranch. Looks brand new, doesn't it?" Sacha handed the pistol to Bob.

"Yep, it looks good as new." Bob said, inspecting it and then handing it back to him. Sacha placed the pistol under his pillow. "Thanks! I need to step out a minute. Be right back!" Bob waited for about twenty minutes, and Sacha didn't return. He reached over to the pistol to look at it again and took it out from under the pillow. He aimed at the floor, pulled the safety back, held the trigger down, and POW! Sacha loaded the pistol by putting a slide in it, and Bob hadn't even noticed! He stared at the floor in alarm, knowing he should've paid more attention.

When it went off, twelve guys were lying around on their cots. When the smoke cleared, they were all gone. Bob sat there in a daze. He laid the gun back on the bunk, and a Marine sergeant thundered up the stairs. Sacha got there first and told Bob to hightail it out of there and run down the back stairs. Bob escaped before the sergeant reached the top of the stairs! Sacha told the sergeant that he was cleaning the gun and it accidently discharged.

About six weeks later, Bob was working in the chow line and the master of arms came up to him and ordered him to put his whites on and report to the captain's mass. The captain's mass is where a person goes before the skipper for any deserved punishment. Bob wasn't sure why he was called, but he knew that you didn't ask questions. You just go.

Bob went as he was instructed and stood in line with six other guys. The captain was telling the other guys they were getting bread and water. When he turned to Bob, he started cussing up a storm. He asked him what kind of person he was to let someone else take the blame for something he had done. Sacha's buddies told the sergeant what really happened. So that made it all the worse. Bob was given five days with bread and water, and he spent time in the brig.

The brig was about six-foot square. He was in there for three days. Twice a day, once in the morning and once in the evening, he was given half a loaf of bread, which was about eight slices. He was not allowed to talk. The third day, somebody pushed old cigarette butts through the hole in the door where they fell on the floor. When the guard opened the door in the afternoon, he saw the cigarettes and said Bob was smoking. Bob was given two more weeks in the brig. The guards were rough. Chet tried to get in to visit, but the guards wouldn't let him in. It was a harsh lesson that Bob never forgot. When he finished his time, he headed back to his seaman's station. Someone had stolen all his clothes and gear. He had to borrow money to replace his things. He learned a hard lesson through that experience: always own up to something you did wrong. It also ended his relationship with the Marines.

Finally, Bob's crew was called out, and one morning they all lined up. His crew was told they were going to take half of the ship's company over to Oakland to go aboard ship. The ship was not finished and still being worked on, but Chet, Whitey, and Bob were among those selected to go to Oakland. So, Bob went aboard his ship for the first time! There were men swarming all over the place on the ship. The men worked round the clock to finish the work.

For the first time, Bob saw they were putting in bunks instead of the hammocks, and they were stacked four high. They were made of steel with a metal mesh underneath. A man couldn't sit up in them and had to duck down. Bob was told to put the mattress he carried in his sea bag over the mesh and was given a couple of blankets. The cubicle he was assigned to held about eighteen men. Right at the end of the bunks was an area about 8 x 12. In that space was a great big diesel engine that took up two decks! That engine ran all the lights on the ship and operated all the time. When he and his friends first sat down in that room, they had to yell to hear each other.

The workers worked all night hammering, banging, and installing guns and all sorts of items all over the ship. The ship had a flight deck that held three aircraft. There was a huge crane on the back that would pick up the seaplanes when they came in on the water. Bob lived there until all the ship company came together, and they were ready to sail in October of 1941.

Chapter 10

A smooth sea never made a skilled sailor.

Franklin D. Roosevelt

After the entire crew reported to the USS *Tangier*, life onboard took on a new rhythm for Bob. There was still time to go on liberty since the United States had not yet entered the war. The USS *Tangier* was docked at Pier 14 in the San Francisco Bay because there were still modifications that the ship needed. They often sailed up the coast to Bremerton, Washington, to the Puget Sound Naval Shipyard and go into dry dock. At the Puget Sound Naval Shipyard, the ship would undergo modifications to make it combat ready. Then routinely the ship would sail back to San Francisco, stopping at Boeing's plant near Aberdeen, Washington. Bob knew this was always hush-hush. He heard that it was one of the sites that were camouflaged—where they built warplanes. West coast warplane plants were often made invisible from the air in case of an imminent attack. Fake towns were built on top of the plants hiding what was taking place below the surface. These fake towns were known as Wonderland. No one would tell the crew where they were going until they were already on their way. Bob and the guys would make guesses, but they were never told or confirmed.

Rumor had it that fighting was close in the Pacific. The Nazi Axis alliance, consisting of Germany, Italy, and Japan threatened to attack Great Britain's naval facility in Singapore and the American military installations in the Philippines. Several British submarines were attacked in the Pacific by the Japanese.

One day, the commander and officers called the crew together and told them they were headed to Pearl Harbor in Honolulu, Hawaii, in the Pacific. It took them about fourteen days to get there. The sea crossing was uneventful, and during the time, everyone was walking on eggshells. Bob thought a lot about his family. There was no telling how long he was going to be away. To keep his mind focused, Bob found ways to get by his homesickness. He volunteered to stand on watch. He stood on watch in the bow where there were seats on both sides, way up in the bow in the high part. When in rough water, Bob had to wear his rain gear. The water used to break over the ship, and he sat there for about four hours with binoculars looking out. Just before the *Tangier* left for Pearl Harbor, the craziest thing happened on ship.

Before the ship set sail, there were still some finishing touches that had to be completed. The orders were to mount the Bofors, 40 mm anti-aircraft guns, in line and sight the targets. That process could only be done in dry dock in a specialized weaponry location and not in the Puget Sound Naval Shipyard. It had to be completed in a controlled environment – they had to "pretend" they were setting the sights of the guns on a specific target in a training exercise. It could not be done on land or outside a large, populated city.

The *Tangier* had been docked at Pier 14 in San Francisco, so before heading to Pearl Harbor, the ship was ordered to sail to Mare Island near San Francisco to mount the Bofors. The *Tangier* left Pier 14 and went to Mare Island. Mare Island was a naval shipyard that did specialty work, including installing the guns and the latest radar on ships. On the way there, the *Tangier* had to go out of Moore Dry Dock in the bay (a ship repair yard) and travel up through the bay into the Carquinez Strait. The Carquinez Strait is eight miles long, and the water is fast flowing.

The *Tangier* headed up the strait to Mare Island and completed the work and then moved out of the dry dock area at Mare Island and anchored out in the Carquinez Strait. The first night, it was Bob's turn on watch. He started the midwatch that began at midnight 0000 and lasted until 4:00 a.m., and it was a dark, clear night sky so Bob could see a good distance. He shared the watch with the ensign, but he was a young guy. Bob was skeptical of the ensign's skills; he didn't come across as having a lot of experience. The ensign was the quarter deck officer that night and Bob's supervising officer during the watch.

Bob stood up on the flight deck toward the aft. He was watching forward as they were swinging around the anchor. The water would flow one way and then the other, and in the strait, the water flowed fast, almost like a sieve, so they were having a hard time and had to keep swinging the anchor around to hold the ship. It was a constant slow swing around the anchor, a full 360-degree circle. Bob was transfixed watching them move the anchor. It looked like a lot of hard work.

During his watch, Bob never noticed anything out of the ordinary other than the guys working hard on the anchor. He became lost in thought about his home in California and wondering how they were doing. He focused his sights on lights out of Frisco and then the Golden Gate Bridge through the mist, thinking different things about his home and family. He kept thinking that he was on his way out to sea, and he didn't really know what was ahead of him or when he was coming back. His watch finished at 4:00 a.m., and he headed back his bunk to get some sleep before he had to get up at 6:30 a.m.

Bob awoke to a great deal of commotion. He was up at 6:30 a.m. but had things to do, so he didn't pay much attention. But while he was eating breakfast in the mess, there was all this noise and shouting outside, guys running and yelling in the passageways. He got up from the table and went topside to find out what was going on. He discovered that during the night while they were swinging around the anchor, it was really dragging anchor. That means the anchor was dragging slowly on the bottom of the strait, making a trench. When it swung around one time, the ship went aground in the sand! For six hours, they had been turning the screw on the bottom of the ship. The screw is the propeller, and the ship would make a *bam, bam, bam, hum, hum, hum* noise while it was hitting the sand and trying to get the ship loose. It was useless, and they were just damaging the shaft. Next, they brought in two tugboats to pull the ship out. That did not work either. The ship was now stuck dead in the middle of the strait!

Bob went to watch the commotion from the flight deck and could see down the strait toward Mare Island. Right away he saw the trouble; there were two destroyers headed toward the *Tangier* and were making steam. They were headed right at the ship at about twenty-five knots, and it was stuck right in their path! Chet met him on the flight deck and told him he heard someone had got this bright idea to direct the destroyers to head toward the ship at full steam and peel off just before they got to the ship, with one destroyer going one direction and the other going the opposite direction. This great big wall of water from their wake hit would hit the *Tangier* on both sides and lift it up! At the same time, the screw would keep working on the bottom of the ship and the tugs would pull. Bob and Chet held on for dear life, and when they opened their eyes, the Tangier shook clear of the sand!

Bob was very skeptical about the whole incident. It happened on his watch and under the supervision of the ensign's watch, and Bob felt the ensign was supposed to be the experienced officer! The ensign and Bob were never was able to live that story down! The crew were told to go to Honolulu, follow their orders, and come back to have the shaft straightened out.

Pearl Harbor, Hawaii, had a reputation of being out of this world. The beaches, the hula girls, and the music mesmerized Bob. He couldn't wait until they were allowed on liberty, which they took when they arrived to base.

Shortly after the initial liberty, the ship was instructed to sail out and around to all the islands. The ship had to go through the process of degaussing, or demagnetizing, to eliminate any remnants of magnetic fields. Magnetized fields in the earth built up magnetics in the ship, and it affected the ship's compasses, or it could even set off a magnetic mine. The crew hung big wires around the top of the ship, and the *Tangier* would sail around the degaussing range house near the peninsula at Pearl City, Honolulu. This was the process of degaussing, or demagnetizing, the ship.

Bob felt like they were going to war, and many men were practicing going through the motions of combat. If the *Tangier* was not degaussing or sailing around the islands, the ship would go out to sea, and the crew would practice shaking all the guns, making sure they were combat ready. During this time, the ship interacted with planes from other ships as they came by towing targets. Targets were like long, soft socks about 18 feet long and about 20 inches in diameter. When the sock or target was pulled by a target tug (aircraft), it filled with air and stuck back; then bombers would practice diving at it, and the ships would fire at it. Bob watched in wonder. There was a 100-foot steel cable between it and the target tug, so he hoped that everyone was shooting at the target and not the plane!

Bob loved the aircraft they worked on and was always asking the pilots to take him flying. Sometimes he flew target tug practice in the Grumman J2 F5 Duck. It was a single-engine plane known as a float airplane. He sat down in the bottom of the bilge on a little seat with a window on each side of him. He had to hand crank the target in and out. He cranked with various sets of hatchet gear. It was a chore. It was easy setting the target out, but it was a chore pulling that target in. Sometimes, he got in so far, he could drop the target out over a ship and let it float down and watch while the sailors below practiced shooting the target before it floated down to the ship. He enjoyed that. The various planes would have different colors during target practice, and the color would let a person know who hit it. Sometimes he and Chet worked together and would throw targets from the ship.

Bob was happy and found that there were lots of opportunities to go ashore. He often hung out at the Royal Hawaiian Hotel in Honolulu, or sometimes he just lay down in the sand on the beach. One afternoon, he passed the pool and plopped down in the sand to stare out to sea. Looking over his shoulder, he could see a sailor sleeping in the sand.

"Hey, Johnny!" he shouted.

Surprise! His friend woke with a start. "Hey, Bobby! I wondered what happened to you! Did you make it all the way out here from San Diego too?"

"It's Bob, not Bobby anymore. Yes, I'm on the USS Tangier. You?"

"I left San Diego not long after you. I'm on the *Vincennes II* cruiser with Tommy from boot camp. We are headed out toward Okinawa," Johnny answered. They talked through the night, and Bobby was glad to catch up with some of the guys from boot camp.

On board the *Tangier*, pilots would come and go. Bob respected the commander; his name was A. F. Sprague. He was tough. Second in command was George De Baun. He was eventually promoted to commander. He smoked a cracked pipe, so Bob always knew when he was around.

During this time, Bob was in the first division of seamen. His division took care of deck work, painted the boats, and did maintenance work. This responsibility as first division seaman lasted about six weeks. Bob's work involved being lowered over the side just above the water. The ship would roll to one side while they were hanging out, and they had to scrape and paint the sides, and, in the process, splashing more paint on themselves than the ship! All this time, he was studying for first class. Jake, the ombudsman, took Bobby under his wing and taught him the knots he struggled with. The Ombudsman served as the mediator between the enlisted men and the officers and encouraged them to learn new trades so that they could advance. Jake and Bobby would go down in the number two hole, a cargo area under the deck, where there was nothing but boxes of rolls of rope and spend two to three hours down there while Bob learned the knots. Bob finally learned how to tie bowlines, sheepshanks, and everything else. Jake gave Bob the first-class seaman's test; Bob passed and was promoted to seaman first class. That was a highlight for Bob!

Bob began to wonder about how he could change divisions too. One day, he was working up under the gas boat on the deck. B Division was the aviation division. A guy in B Division was there working on one of the gas boats, and he was laughing at Bob. He said Bob was too serious and deep in thought. Bob recognized him as Whitey. They had met earlier, but now they became good friends. Whitey convinced Bob to go out for the B division. He suggested Bob strike out for the prop shop, and he offered to talk to somebody to arrange an apprenticeship. Bob's idea was to go straight for mechanic. But the aviation officer intervened and told him he could never get anywhere working with the low guys. He said to check out the metal shop. Bob went to the metal shop as a temporary assignment (TAD) and never looked back. He loved it!

Whitey and Bob began hanging out together. He didn't see much of Chet anymore since he changed jobs. Whitey and Bob played cards and met girls. Bob figured out quickly that the more he wrote girls, the more letters he would get back. He soon figured out he could carbon copy his letters and send the same letter to each girl. Then he shared this idea with Whitey, and they both began writing every girl they met!

In December, one Saturday night, a lot of the ships went out—two carriers at least and a few others. Bob knew they were due to go out, but they didn't get orders this time. Four or five of the men in Bob's Division were sent over to Ford Island to be caretakers to some of the planes that were under repair. Bob was sent with them. A few of the planes were under repair, and Bob assumed they wanted to be sure men from the crew were on hand to do the needed work. So, he was put up in quarters in transit on the naval base and assigned to a bunk.

Out of the four sent over to the base, one played harmonica. His name was Beaver. He was good at the little instrument. About 4:00 p.m., Bob, Beaver, and the other two crew members decided to head over into Pearl Harbor, hit the beach, and do some window shopping. While they were walking around, Beaver went into a music store, found a new harmonica, and bought it. He was trying it out while they were walking on the beach until someone ran up and excitedly told them there was big dance getting ready to start. The guys knew if they went, they could meet a lot of girls, especially if Beaver brought his harmonica along. Some dances were held by the United Services Organization, (USO), and this one was taking place in a park over by Diamond Head next to the aquarium. The USO entertained the troops by holding dances and other social events. Bob saw hula girls dancing in hula skirts. Bob paid twenty-five cents to pose with a hula girl for a picture. The dancers were good, and Bob always had fun dancing with them. He'd been to dances a few times before, but it was always by chance, not his original intention.

There were guys from the other ships docked on the same base, and this time, the USO was holding a dance contest. Bob stayed until about midnight then took the motor launch back to base. All in all, Bob was settling into navy life. He decided Pearl Harbor was not the worst place to be.

Chapter 11

No man can tame a tiger into a kitten by stroking it.

Franklin D. Roosevelt, December 8, 1941

A few days later, on December 7, 1941, Bob was startled awake with a huge explosion that shook his whole building. His bunk was about fifteen feet from the nearest window. He stumbled over to it half-asleep, looked out, and saw the number one hangar full of smoke. Fire was billowing out of it! He turned to his bunkmates and hollered that a plane had hit the hangar. When he turned back around, he saw a plane overhead with big red balls on the wings. His first thought was that it was a Russian bomber. He shouted, "The Russians are attacking!" By then, the other guys were jumping up and grabbing gear and clothes.

The reason Bob thought it was an airplane that hit the hangar was because air patrols left out of that hangar every morning. They would return around sunset and taxi close to that hangar and sometimes fly right over it. He first thought one of those props had hit the hangar because those planes carried about thirteen hours of gasoline and sometimes ran short on their way back in and had to make a quick landing. He thought for sure that was what happened.

Bob's quarters were on the second floor, and he had not heard any orders following the explosion. He reached for his whites and grabbed his gear anyway. Bob pulled on his pants and undershirt and slapped his hat on. He didn't take time to put on his top at that point but grabbed his shoes as he ran out the door. He raced down the first set of steps and then sat in the stairwell to put on his shoes. When he stepped off the landing and opened the door and to look outside, he saw the other guys from his crew had gone on ahead of him. Then he saw these men breaking all the windows in front of the barracks.

This didn't make any sense to Bob. He was in a daze and saw these guys using broom handles to break every window. All he could hear around himself were explosions that appeared to be coming from everywhere. Everything was chaotic. Bob strode forward.

A sailor yelled to everyone, "All you men come with me!" Bob was in a stupor. He didn't ask questions and just followed the man.

The sailor was quick, too, as he led Bob and the other guys who were running down the street past the swimming pool. Bob looked toward the sky and saw planes flying over, but he couldn't make out what was happening. There was too much haze from the smoke. The sailor led the group over to the armory, and someone had set boxes of rifles, gas masks, and ammunition out in piles on the grass. Another sailor was handing them out to everybody. An officer grabbed Bob by the arm, threw a bandolier over his shoulder, and handed him a rifle and a gas mask. Then the officer turned and grabbed another guy behind Bob too. He turned back to Bob, looked him in the eye, and said, "Do you know how to use this?" Bob nodded yes. He pointed Bob to a building and said, "You see that administration building? I want you to go up to the top and out on to the roof."

Bob quickly followed the orders, and the two ran down the street and over to the building. Inside it was a madhouse. This building was right where all the carriers came in to tie up. It was the naval operations building. Bob asked for the stairway to the roof, and they ran to the top. The guy with him had no clothes on, but he was wrapped in a Marine officer's white coat. He was a young guy, about the same age as Bob. He asked, "Do you know how to load this?"

"Are you kidding me? You should know more about this than I do—you're a Marine!" Bob showed him how to load it and put the clip down into it.

There was a small cement building up right in the middle of the roof where they kept buckets, mops, and cleaning supplies. The roof was gravel with a wall all the way around it, a little lower than waist high. It was about 30 inches high and a foot thick. What Bob saw when he looked out over the edge would never be erased from his memory. There were Japanese aircraft flying everywhere—over tops of buildings and ships and even right over top of him on the building. A quick thought pierced Bob's mind. Somewhere down there was the *Tangier*, but he didn't know where. He was hoping his ship was still out at sea.

There were bombs sliding out of the aircraft and falling down at crazy angles. Bob could see them sliding down toward the ships. In his mind, it was like slow motion. There was so much smoke and fire that it was hard to make out the shapes of the ships, but he could see the ships' masts. He looked out from the navy yard toward the point and then to Diamond Head. There were just no words to describe it. Bob would tell people later in life that the scene was etched in his memory. He could not look away and stood transfixed in horror.

As the planes circled around surrounding the island, Bob and the other men on the roof would duck down behind the cement shack because the planes were firing at them as they flew over. The men would let them fire as they whizzed over their heads. Then Bob and the other men would come out from around the building and shoot at them with all they had. The planes were so low Bob could see the Japanese sitting in the back in the greenhouse, the bubble observation canopy on the top of the Japanese fighter aircraft. They were so close that Bob thought if he had grenades, he could've hit them.

When they stopped coming their way, Bob saw the destroyer *Shaw* in the dry dock. He watched it take a direct hit from one of the bombers. The bombs landed in front of the bridge of the ship. The destroyer lifted clean up out of the dry dock and made a great leaping flip. He watched a ship called the *Okinawa* being blasted by bombs. Two Marines came running up to the roof with boxes and set up a 50-caliber machine gun. The Marines set it up and were firing like crazy men at the planes. This big gun was supposed to be a water-cooled machine gun, but they had no water. After a while, Bob could see the bullets from the gun corkscrewing, and the barrel glowed with heat. But the soldiers weren't about to stop.

Bob watched in disbelief as the *West Virginia*, the *Tennessee*, and the *California* got hit. The *California* was almost directly below him.

This day changed Bob's life. He witnessed so many men killed that day. He survived because he was lucky. Bombs were dropping and exploding all around him. The *California* directly below him was destroyed as well as the ships beside it. How the building he stood on never was bombed, he would never know. Bob guessed luck was just with him that day.

The attack lasted one hour and 15 minutes but since it was so chaotic, Bob didn't have much sense of the time. After heavy fighting which seemed to last hours, a Marine officer came up to the roof and brought some more soldiers with him. He told Bob that he was relieved and to go to the mess hall to eat something. There had been too much happening to feel any hunger, but Bob and the other Marine who was wearing only the white coat headed down the stairs to find the mess hall. When they walked into the hall, all Bob could see were bodies piled everywhere. The mess hall had been turned into a hospital and morgue. Bodies were brought in from where they had fallen and they were stacked on tables. On one side of the hall, they were serving some kind of chicken plate, and Bob knew he couldn't swallow any of it.

The day of the attack was a madhouse. Fresh water was brought in from Honolulu on a regular basis but since the attack decimated the ships in the harbor, the navy feared losing the water supply. For a period of time, Bob was assigned to guard the swimming pool in case it would be used for drinking water. Word circulated that the Japanese enemy warships were on their way and an attack was imminent. Bob and the surviving men were all on notice. He was given side arms and assigned to different duties. His assignment changed several times during the next day and evening.

Bob was finally sent along with a few other guys down to the hangars that faced where the carriers sank. There were 20-millimeter and 40-millimeter gun mounts set up, and he was assigned one of those guns. There were four big guns altogether, and they had sandbags stacked surrounding them. He was told he had to stay there until he was relieved.

Bob's job was to man the 20-millimeter munition cartridges. They were in an oblong case, and when one case was emptied, he detached it and put another one in place. Everyone was on edge since the word was an attack was forthcoming. They were told when enemy planes were sighted, the fire siren would go off. Bob and the men would tense up waiting for the siren to sound. He swore you could hear that siren all over the island. Their orders were not to commence shooting until the siren went off, and then they would shoot at whatever they saw.

At one point, Bob was relieved, and he went down to the hangar with another guy to where the planes from the *Tangier* were parked outside the hangar, the one hanger that was not hit. Bob wanted to know if they could pull the planes in because they were damaged. The planes were hit with big pieces of concrete where the bombs had landed on the ramp and the concrete flew into the air, raining down on the planes. The horizontal stabilizer was damaged on one plane, and the other one's wing was hit. Bob hoped to get at least one plane working, so the plan was to pull the horizontal stabilizer off one and put it on the one that was damaged. Bob was told the enemy was coming back, and he was to work to get as many planes as he could into the air. He and the other guys were trying to fix the planes and get them in the hangar so they could be repaired as quickly as possible.

Later the same evening, Bob was eventually sent back down to his station. He had lost sense of time and didn't know what time it was except that it was dark. He heard some airplanes coming, so he raced into place and looked out to the right toward Diamond Head. The enemy planes had come in that way, past Honolulu and into Ford Island. He saw blinking lights, formation lights, and they were blinking on and off. The planes drew close and then somebody—Bob did know who it was—but somebody out in the bay started firing. After that first shot, the next fire was a tracer. Tracers were red to help someone see where to fire and aim. The tracers have bright lights so that a shooter would know if he was right on target. By watching the tracer every ship opened fire!

There were about six planes shot down that night. No one knew what they were firing at. There so many explosions Bob thought he would scream, and no one could hear anything because it was so loud. Bob felt like it lasted a long time. In the height of the firestorm, someone came running and told Bob and the men at the guns to take cover. Some other guys had cut a trench across the end of the runway, and everyone ran over and jumped into it. Bob didn't. He stayed behind the sand-bags with a couple of other guys.

The siren never sounded. They were US airplanes! They were signaling their lights so that they could land. They were from the USS *Enterprise*. Word was one of the merchant ships out in the bay was spooked and took the first shot. Bob thought everyone was killed in the six planes but heard later some were rescued.

Bob was not ashamed to say that he was scared. In truth, Bob was so scared he couldn't stand up straight, so he put his knees on the sandbag while he used his cannon on the 20-millimeter gun mount. He didn't know who the guys were with him, and he didn't know who he was shooting at. The next morning, he found out the Japanese never came. After the Japanese attacked, they turned tail and flew off.

Chapter 12

The eyes of the world are upon you.

Dwight D. Eisenhower

Bob spent the next several days on Ford Island, waiting for orders to return to the *Tangier*. During that time, he learned several facts about the attack. The Japanese launched their attack two hundred miles from Oahu off six Japanese aircraft carriers. They launched forty-three dive-bombers and twenty-four torpedo planes from an altitude of sixty feet. The ships that were docked in Pearl Harbor were the primary targets for the first wave of bombers, and eighteen warships were sunk or heavily damaged. Over 2,400 military men were killed in contrast to sixty-four Japanese. One of the many grisly scenes replaying over and over in Bob's seventeen-year-old mind was the one of the men jumping off the USS *California* and trying to swim away while being burned by the flames on the water. Looking down from his place on the roof, there wasn't anything Bob could do but shoot and shoot as the Japanese aircraft flew off in all directions during the attack.

It was several days before Bob was called back to the *Tangier*. When he boarded his ship, he learned that the gunners on the *Tangier* were responsible for downing three enemy aircraft and causing severe damage to a midget submarine that stealthily snuck its way into the harbor. Bob was proud of the gunners and made a special trip to congratulate them. Bob knew he shot hundreds of rounds, but he never knew if he hit anything.

Since the *Tangier* was one of the few ships not damaged, their orders came quickly. News was received that the Japanese's next target was Wake Island; in fact, it was already under siege. The ship was ordered to head immediately to Wake Island and rendezvous with a carrier, the USS *Saratoga*, and deliver supplies. Even though the weather was mild, Bob sweated as he lugged the much-needed supplies onto his ship. His country was now at war! The shock of the attack had not dissipated, and the reality of an altered future left him feeling disoriented. Bob knew it would take a long time, if ever, to return to normalcy. Patriotism mixed with a frantic energy to support their country, along with a lot of fear for the future, served as adrenaline for many of the youngest members of the navy, of which Bob was one.

It wasn't long before the USS *Tangier* met up with the USS *Saratoga*. As the convoy headed toward Wake Island, they received word that the Japanese overran the island, and the US troops were forced to surrender. The *Tangier* was ordered to report back to Oahu where they were to assist in cleanup until their next assignment. Soon after they reported back, they received orders to head to New Caledonia to tender Catalina airplanes. The USS *Tangier* was moved in to replace the

USS *Curtiss*, one of the navy's first seaplane tenders. Bob was back to doing what he loved most—a mechanic serving seaplanes and meeting new people.

While in New Caledonia, the *Tangier* participated in many long-range search missions. Bob was always interested in learning anything new and was anxious to find out firsthand what was happening in other parts of the Pacific. Talking with the pilots who were having their planes serviced, Bob learned of an impending battle to occur in the Coral Sea. Sure enough, the *Tangier* received six more planes to service in preparation for the battle.

When the Battle of the Coral Sea began in May 1942, Bob was once more thrust into a battle. This battle lasted four days. It was a win for the Allies! The Japanese were prevented from gaining more Pacific territory. This was the first time the Japanese retreated without gaining ground in the war. For Bob and the men on the seaplane tender, the *Tangier* was not actively involved in combat. A destroyer, the USS *Slim*, and an oiler, the USS *Neosho*, were sunk. Bob, along with his crew, spent long days and nights rescuing men from the sinking ships and bringing them back to safety.

Bob felt strong emotions when saving a sailor from a sure death in the ocean. To keep their minds clear and to fight the fear of the unknown, Bob and the crew shared stories of successful rescues or memories of friends that were lost in the attack when taking a break from duty. Honestly, most of the men were relieved that their ship was not engaged in battle. Bob often felt the powerful emotional pull of war and the brevity of life and death. He would never see things through his prewar lens again. Bob experienced so much in that past year. He vowed to always work hard and do his best at whatever task was assigned to him. He already established a good work ethic from his father; the experiences from 1942 cemented it into the man Bob would become. It can be said that one defining moment can shape life, and the experience of Pearl Harbor and the following battles defined the view from which Bob would approach his adult life choices and decisions.

When the search for survivors ended, the *Tangier*'s airplanes returned to patrol the Pacific until the USS *Curtiss* arrived in July to replace them. Bob's ship was reassigned to Espiritu Santo to support the Catalina planes stationed there. Compared to New Caledonia, Espiritu Santo was paradise. It was a small island located in the New Hebrides Islands in the South Pacific. Following the Pearl Harbor attack, it was decided that this small island would be the perfect spot to build a large naval base. Even though the island was defended by US troops, the threat from the Japanese was thought to be minimal. The island remained safe throughout the war.

When Bob arrived in Espiritu Santo, he discovered a dense jungle behind a bay with lots of small island huts lining the beach. Bob stepped onto the beach and drew in a breath of fresh air. He felt a release from all the tense months behind him. Since his primary role was to support the Catalina planes, a job he enjoyed, he found he had lots of free time. After a few weeks on the island, he and the crew built a baseball diamond to play ball between shifts. It was a great way to pass the time.

The natives on the island taught the sailors how to climb trees to pick coconuts. Some of the men used the coconut to make hemp; although Bob loved the coconut meat and juice, he discovered that coconuts were quite the laxative! Bob saw few women on the island. He learned that most of the women were moved into the hills when the navy arrived to start building the base. Most of the women he saw were good looking and friendly, so he understood why they wanted to keep them separated.

At one point, the military provided a jeep to the men of the *Tangier* so they could travel to a nearby airstrip. The airstrip was located high in the mountains, about an hour from where they were docked. The trip through the jungle was interesting, and Bob repeatedly asked to be on the crew heading to the airstrip. From his station on the airstrip, he could see everywhere around the island. He noticed the lush jungle was a contrast to the mountains in Southern California. He saw waterfalls streaming off the mountains to form small clear pools of water. Dark green vines grew all over, covered with the most beautiful fragrant flowers he had ever seen. Each time he traveled to the airstrip; he was reminded of the scenery in all the tropical movies he watched. Only now he could see in color! The best times were when he and his friends would stop and swim in the pools of water.

One day when Bob was at the airfield to pick up some parts for repairs, he saw several black pilots that had flown in with an Air Force crew. Since Bob had never seen African American pilots and only saw blacks in positions such as cooks or other behind the scenes maintenance jobs, he wanted to talk to the airmen. He met one of the pilots and reached out to shake his hand.

Bob shared his questions with the pilot, and the pilot laughed. "Son, we are a government experiment. Bob, not understanding what the man meant, asked for more information. Bob listened intently as the man explained how he came to be a pilot as a part of the Tuskegee airmen. He told Bob it started with a visit from the first lady, Eleanor Roosevelt, who visited Alabama and flew in an airplane with one of the first black pilots. From that point, he explained, a training institute for black men was established, and black men were recruited to be airmen and pilots. He told Bob it was not only pilots who were trained but also bombardiers and gunners and a slew of other positions. The pilot said he really didn't know where he would end up fighting because the first group had just been assigned to active duty. The men coming from his training camp were dispersed into many different units. This was only a quick stop before heading to a destination in Europe.

On the way back to the tender, Bob thought about what the pilot had told him about the program. The pilot had also spoke about how bad discrimination was for blacks in the South. Bob was very familiar with discrimination. He grew up on the wrong side of the tracks in the desert. He remembered that there were times when he was young when he had to sit in a tent outside of the school because he looked like a Mexican. Bob hoped the airman would be able to return to his family safely after the war. Later in life, Bob read about the Tuskegee airmen and believed he met one of the first.

Espiritu Santo had yet another airfield for the Sea-bees' B-24 squadron. A camp was set up across the bay from where Bob's crew were assigned. The Seabees would often come in late at night with their planes smoking and all shot up. Bob and his friends would sit on the beach, watching with binoculars, as they came and went. One night, the men of the *Tangier* were invited to a beer party held for one of the Seabees' ships. Everyone in Bob's crew went to the party. Bob heard that the beer was do-nated by some popular beer companies like Lucky Lager and ABC. The beer was placed in huge drums with the tops cut off. When Bob first arrived, he saw the beer was in bottles, sitting on a pallet, and were most likely hot. Looking around, he didn't see any ice. He shook his head and decided it really didn't matter; he was going to drink the beer even if it was warm.

Before Bob could get to the beer, he saw some of the Seabee crew posting no smoking signs all around. Curi-ous, Bob found a spot to watch as the sailors placed the bottles in the drums, covered the beer in the tubs with 115-octane aviation gasoline, and then pumped air into the barrels. The gasoline would bubble up and frost the bottles! Dangerous, sure, but it was good! Bob drank his share that night.

During his time on the island, he made second class metal smith. Bob always wanted to move up in the navy and was pleased he was able to attain a new rank. While they were stationed there, Bob and his friends would constantly check orders to see if anyone was sent back to the States or transferred to a different ship. One time an order came in for a second-class metal smith, and one of his friends, Morris, received orders to go to New Construction. New Construction was a term for constructing battalions. During the war if assigned to New Construction, it meant the serviceman would be sent to active combat zones to work, anywhere anyplace. This meant Morris would be assigned to another ship and head back out to sea once more. Morris did not want to go, and he begged Bob to take his place. He even offered Bob $50 if he would trade places. Bob thought about it, but he did not want to go to New Construction, so he put Morris off, and Morris kept pestering him about the offer.

Shortly after Morris received orders, Bob's closest friends, Whitey and Rio, received transfer orders. A rumor began to circulate that the *Tangier* was going to the Philippines and then Australia. Bob began to seriously think about taking Morris's offer. Bob finally agreed, took the $50, and changed the name on the order to state he volunteered to take Morris's place. Bob did not know it then, but the *Tangier* was sent back to San Diego to be overhauled. After the overhaul, the *Tangier* traveled back to Espiritu Santo on its way to Brisbane and then to New Guinea to support General MacArthur.

Shortly after turning in his order, the USS *Chandeleur* arrived in Espiritu Santo with final orders for Bob and his friends. Bob, Whitey, and Rio left the island and returned to Oakland, California, with the USS *Chandeleur*. It took them three weeks to travel by ship and then by bus from Oakland to San Diego. Bob and his friends immediately reported In and were surprised that they had been given three weeks' liberty. What a break! The guys did not waste any time taking liberty in San Diego.

One evening when they returned from the city, they were told they each had to have a private interview with the commander. Bob wondered what was going on and immediately began to grow nervous. When it was Bob's turn to meet the commander, he learned that the commander was not so bad. He was friendly and candid. He told Bob that he made it a habit to personally know the men he had to assign placement. Standing ramrod straight in front of the commander, Bob watched as the man reviewed his papers.

"So, you were at Pearl Harbor?" the commander asked.

Bob replied, "Yes, sir!"

The commander added, "You have been out there a long time, haven't you?"

Bob replied, "Yes, sir!" wondering where this conversation was headed. The commander's tone was concerned but undemanding.

The commander continued, "Listen, we normally assign men a specific place to go, but instead, I want to give you a choice. Hell, I want to give you three choices." The commander rattled off two ships and an air station with a squadron he could choose. Bob's mind was working quickly. He was trying to figure out which choice had the best chance of keeping him from going back out to sea. His experience on the island was fine, but it was lonely, and the memories of Pearl were too fresh.

That was the danger of choosing New Construction. The navy was quickly building new ships, and he figured he would just be sent out again. He wasn't sure he was ready. Bob then remembered a guy on the *Tangier* who always talked about place he was stationed at one time near Washington, DC. The guy had told him it was a great place for duty, and it was near Fort Meyers where aviation first began. Bobby didn't know the first thing about the place, but he blurted out, "Anacostia?"

"Sure," replied the commander, nodding his head, "that will be a good place for you." And that is where Bob was assigned. Three days later, Bob received his orders for Anacostia Naval Air Station. He also found they were delayed orders, giving him another thirty days. He was free to go wherever he wanted.

Bob had saved a little money, about $700, from his flight payments. He had some of it in cash and some in checks that he stashed in his wallet. Whitey and Rio received different orders and were already headed out of town, so Bob was alone. He checked in to a little hotel and cleaned himself up for a night on the town. His first stop was in a bar. He ordered a bottle of the beer and headed back to the washroom. When he returned to his seat, he finished his beer and left. When he arrived back in his hotel, he reached for his wallet, and it was gone! Bob could not find it.

He went back to the lobby desk and told the clerk. He remembered thinking on his way back from the bar he would stop for a cup of coffee and thought he felt for his wallet in his pocket but didn't actually stop for the coffee. The clerk had not seen the wallet. Bob then walked back to the bar and spoke with the bartender. The bartender had not seen anything. Bob checked the restroom and walked back and forth across the park, trying to retrace his steps. Bob was devastated. His month-long liberty would be horrible without any money.

Walking into the hotel lobby, Bob saw the clerk waving at him. The clerk called to him, "Hey, buddy, I have a note for you. I think some guy wants you to meet him at his trailer court somewhere." The clerk eyed him carefully. "You better be careful. Just sayin'."

Bob had an uneasy feeling about this, but he was hoping the guy might have his wallet and money. Bob replied, "I need that money, so I am going to see him. You have the address if I don't come back." Bob went outside and hailed a cab.

It was late and dark, which made the whole scene ominous. Bob felt uneasy as they drove into a part of town he had not been to before. When they reached the trailer court, he asked the cab driver to wait while he went up to the door. He knocked on the thin screen door, his mind imagining all sorts of horrible things, and the door was suddenly sprung open wide by a wrinkled old Italian man who was smiling and laughing.

The man spoke in broken English, "Come in! Come in! I've been waiting for you!"

Bob did not want to go inside until he found out what was going on. "What are you doing and what do you want?" Bob asked more fiercely than he felt.

The man looked around Bob, waved the taxi off, and quietly said, "Come in!"

Seeing that he had little choice and he needed his money, Bob went in and sat at the table. The man took a picture and laid it on the table.

"Is this your wife?" the man asked.

"I am not married," stated Bob. Looking closer at the picture, Bob realized it was a picture from his wallet of his stepmother, Audra. At that point, Bob knew the man had his wallet, so he decided to play along. Bob soon learned that the man had not been in the States long and was an airplane mechanic who worked in the city in San Diego. After they talked a while, the man gave Bob the wallet back. Bob checked, and the man had not taken anything out of it. All the money and the checks were still in place. Bob tried to give the old man $20, but he wouldn't take it. The man told Bob that he wanted to give the wallet back personally because he didn't trust anyone. Bob figured the man was just lonely and wanted someone to talk to. Bob reasoned that he still had a few days before he traveled to El Centro to visit his family, so he promised to come back and visit the old man several times. They became friends. Bob was also very careful with his wallet after that night.

A week later, Bob bought a ticket to El Centro and took the bus back home for a few days. He went out on a few dates with girls he knew from high school, and Raul treated him to an Eagles game. Raul took off work a few days, and the two of them went to Los Angeles to meet some of Raul's union friends. By now, Bob had some ribbons on his chest, and Raul was proud to show off his son. When it was time for Bob to leave, he said his goodbyes to his family and walked down to the El Centro train station. He had three days to travel to Anacostia in Washington, DC, and to report for duty. It was many years before Bob went back to El Centro to see his family. He had a family of his own the next time his saw his dad.

Chapter 13

Be Brave. Take risks. Nothing can substitute experience.

Paulo Coelho

Bob reported to duty at Anacostia Naval Base, Washington, DC, in 1943 as a second-class metal smith. He was assigned to the metalsmith shop, and his duties included welding, wing work, and odd repairs. These duties were a breeze for Bob. It was what he liked to do most. Whenever a plane had an accident and came in for repair, he would be called to the field do the repair work. He couldn't be happier about his vocation.

In Anacostia, Bob saw the end of WWII and moved right into the Cold War as the age of jet aviation, radar, and electronics took center stage. Bob was not one to ponder on the political state of the world. He was right in the middle of the budding new era, and he loved it. His experience at Pearl Harbor changed him, in a good way. It was a defining moment in his life, making him stronger and determined to hold onto the honorable things in life and to let go of those things that overshadowed the good. In later life Bob often received letters from retired service men in their eighties and nineties that bemoaned about their past decisions and life mistakes. Bob did not want to be like them, and he often stated that you should learn from challenging experiences not cry about them.

Although Bob was excited about his new roles, adjusting to the East Coast was not as easy as he thought it would be. He battled homesickness. During this time his family often wrote to him, it was tough for him not being able to see them in person. It wasn't too long before the letters turned bitter with talk of harsh family matters, and everyone pushed him to take a side. Bob just now learned that due to Raul and Jessie's scandalous divorce, his father finding himself with many children, quickly remarried. Bob's siblings did not have a good relationship with their new stepmother, and it seemed as if relationship issues disrupted their lives daily.

Depression soon set in every time he received a letter from home. He knew there was nothing he could do from the East Coast to help in any way, and he did not want to get in the middle of family disputes. Occasionally, he would receive a letter from Jessie. Having left Raul, she was now living in Ohio and working at a flea market. She sent Bob photographs of herself and her son, Billy—Bob's younger stepbrother. This came as a surprise. Bob never really knew what to say to his mother. He had not seen her since his parents' divorce, and her letters called for his sympathy in some of the family's arguments. He eventually sent a couple of letters to his father but made a point to keep things light and never gave any advice. There was a time when he just stopped answering the letters. As he became involved in his new life in Washington, DC, he drifted away from his family when he realized he had to let them go. There were many other things going on in Bob's life and he knew he needed to focus on the present.

Bob felt like his work in Anacostia was the best thing going. There were many opportunities to use his skills and learn new ones. He spent the majority of his time working inside the various hangers. He and his crew would turn out about fifty planes a day by starting them and prepping them for the pilots. Some days, he would taxi the planes in and out of the hangar.

One day, Bob was working with one of the navy trainer planes, 30 SNJs. His leader tapped him on the shoulder and told him to taxi it out. This was time consuming to set up because the plane had to be attached to a tractor and pulled out of the hangar, but Bob was excited to have this chance. Once it was out, he was trying to get the plane over several blocks that formed a makeshift ramp. He tried and tried to get the plane over the ramp without success. His crew would push the plane in place, but he always fell back.

Bob's leader, Doug, yelled, "Bob! Give it more throttle!"

After a few attempts, Bob decided he would really throttle it one more time. The plane flew over the blocks so fast he couldn't stop the plane until it was twelve inches from the door of the fire station on the opposite side of the field! They found him standing up with his feet on the brakes while the firemen were running out of the station. Unfortunately, Bob did not live this incident down, and it was the last time he was allowed to taxi the planes out.

While he was working on the day shift, an incident occurred in the Potomac River, right outside the base. The incident involved a Grumman G-44 Widgeon seaplane. The seaplane would taxi up and down the Potomac River between the naval air station and the Alexandria gun factory.

One day while it was preparing to taxi to Alexandria, the plane hit a huge log in the water.

There were three men on board, and the log turned up and went straight through the bottom of the plane all the way into the cockpit. The seaplane quickly began sinking. Fortunately, the Coast Guard was able to save the men, but the seaplane was badly damaged. The plane was pulled up and brought in for repairs. Bob spent six months putting that plane back together.

Eventually he moved to the night shift. The night crew worked on the planes that flew each day. He was able to learn all about electronics on this shift and was glad to take on the new responsibilities. Each night, he and the new crew would asscss the planes that came in with electronical issues because they had to be ready to go out the next day. The radios were one of the main issues at night. Being a quick learner, he mastered the electronic systems to all the planes at the airbase in a matter of days.

The night shift held all sorts of benefits for Bob. As the war ended, gasoline was still being rationed in Washington, DC, during this time. Cars had to have an A, B, or C sticker in order to get gas. He found that using the letter and some stamps, the crews at the base could fill their cars overnight. Sometimes he would even trade his flight jackets for gas at the station.

In addition to his mechanic duties, Bob was required to do flight time. Flight time was required for anyone working with the instrument panel of aircraft. He often traveled with the pilots to offer mechanical assistance. Since he was not a pilot, he would go down to the operations buildings and find a pilot to take him out. One day, Bob ran into Commander Anderson, chief of operations.

Anderson called to him, "Hey, Bob, do you want to fly with me in the SNJ?"

Thinking it was a good deal to fly with the commander, Bob excitedly said, "Yes, sir!"

They suited up and climbed into the aircraft. Bob eyed the dashboard. He sat behind the pilot and looked out the window over the capitol grounds as they began their climb. They flew all around over Virginia and into Maryland.

They were over Hyde Field in Maryland when Anderson spoke up. "Hey, Bob, mind if I do some touch and goes?" Bob knew this was an exercise pilots used to practice their landings. He gave the commander a thumbs-up, and the commander smiled broadly. "Hang on!"

When the plane came down for a landing, Bob heard the wind catch the rudder. Anderson began cussing up a storm, and Bob was sure they were going to crash because the plane flew straight up, cartwheeled, and headed for the ground. Anderson managed to land the plane, but when they got out of the cockpit, they saw that one wing was damaged. Anderson was still cussing and stressing about how they would get back to base. Meanwhile, Bob was circling the plane and accessing the damage.

"I can fix this, sir," said Bob.

Anderson gaped at Bob. "How?"

"Well," began Bob, "we can take the wing tip off and fly back without the tip. I can rig it up enough to make it back." That is what they did. Commander Anderson helped Bob, and they made an uneventful trip back to base. No one ever questioned the commander or noticed anything wrong with the plane. The following day, Bob repaired the wing, and no one ever knew what happened. After that, Anderson always kept an eye out for Bob.

Not long after that experience, a new aircraft arrived in Anacostia. It was a Cessna Bobcat made of fabric and wood. Most of the planes at the air station were made of metal. No one on the crew had experience working with this type of plane, so Bob volunteered to take it on since he had worked with wood when he was on the USS *Tangier*. The commander took him up on his offer and sent Bob away to school for six weeks for Cessna training. He came back an expert.

Secretary of the Navy James Forrestal kept his personal plane at Anacostia. He had a R50 Lockheed Hudson that he would come over and fly from time to time. The secretary had his own private crew, and they kept the Hudson in perfect shape. One morning, his crew was preparing to taxi his plane out, and suddenly, a tire blew out. It was always a big to-do when an officer like that was on base, so everyone on base was standing there watching, including Bob. He knew it was a task to change the tire because you had to take the brake assembly off to change it and then put it back on. It was a big chore, and the secretary was in a big hurry.

Suddenly, one of Bob's crew, Juan, ran forward and said, "I can do it, sir...in ten minutes!"

The secretary stared at him for a long minute and then told him to have at it. Ten minutes later, the secretary walked over to Juan and patted him on the back. Bob couldn't believe his eyes! It was ready, and the secretary didn't lose any time. Juan made first class mechanic on the spot! Bob took it to heart and told himself to never hesitate, do your best work, and learn to be a risk taker.

Not all of Bob's days at Anacostia were pleasant. Bob had already experienced the death and destruction at Pearl Harbor, and there were always accidents with planes and their pilots. One afternoon, Bob was sitting up in the rafters of the hangar working and occasionally watching the planes landing and taxiing in. There was so much noise from the planes and the machinery that he had a hard time hearing anything. Bob stared as a man started walking across the runway where the planes were landing. The guy was intently focused on some cards in his hand and didn't notice a Beechcraft airplane coming in for a landing. The Beechcraft has a high nose so the man could not see the plane in his peripheral vision and kept walking. Bob saw everyone yelling to the man to stop, but with all the noise, the man couldn't hear anyone. He walked right into the blades that caught him on the shoulder and threw him under the plane. The blade cut his arm in four or five places and tore up his hip. Bob learned that he was going to be in Bethesda Hospital for a long time. When he did return to the base a year later, he could no longer use that arm. Even though it was a terrible accident, Bob knew the man was lucky.

Once on a carrier in the Pacific, he saw a parachutist walk into a prop, and it cut the top half of his body off. Bob learned early to stay away from the propellers.

Another accident Bob witnessed was when a B-25 Mitchell bomber flew into Bolling Airforce Base. Bob was out on the runway working on a plane and watched as the bomber came in too long for the runway, overshooting it, and ended up sliding into the airfield on the grass. As the plane was sliding, he watched in amazement as six men rolled out of the plane while it was still sliding. No one was injured!

It wasn't long before Bob met Arthur Godfrey at Anacostia. Godfrey was a commander in the Army Reserves and flew a TBM torpedo bomber. Godfrey wanted to fly in the Winchester Apple Blossom Festival that was held in Virginia each spring. His idea was to fly his plane from Leesburg, Virginia, to Anacostia with the hope that someone would be able to rig his plane so he could drop apple blossoms over the parade in Winchester. Bob and one his friends, Joe, were assigned to assist Godfrey. Bob and Joe worked overnight to take the guns out of the plane and make a chute to fit in the empty space. Once they got it working, they had several practice runs with the pilot before they tried it with Godfrey.

Bob cut up a whole bunch of paper to give it a try. They went out over the Chesapeake Bay with their bags of paper. The first time they attempted a drop, something went wrong, and all of the paper flew back into the inside of the plane. The pilot was screaming he couldn't see! Bob laughed at the sight. He thought it looked like there was a bunch of snow falling inside the airplane. After making several adjustments and a few more practice drops, the plane was ready to go. Bob and Joe flew with Godfrey to the parade. As the plane flew low over the parade route, Bob fed apple blossoms down the chute, and they floated down on the parade. Watching the pink and white petals floating down, Bob thought this was the most beautiful thing he had ever seen.

Bob was eager to make first class and studied for the test during most of his free time. One night in town, he met his first wife, Anne. She was a pretty woman who worked for a law office in Washington, DC. She was from a small town in North Carolina and had a slew of beautiful sisters. They married in 1944 and rented a small apartment in Washington, DC.

Bob knew he had to decide about his life in the navy. He had reached a point where he had to sign on for another four years or leave the navy. He knew if he signed on again, there was a good chance he would be sent back out to sea. Now that he had married Anne, he did not want to do that.

Shortly after he and Anne were settled, Bob told his commanding officer about his dilemma. He told him that he liked the base and working where he was, but he had just gotten married and didn't want to go back out to sea.

"Bob," the officer said to him, "why don't you try the TAR program? It is a Navy Reserve program."

"I do not want the reserves," he answered quickly. This did not appeal to Bob, and he believed the reserves would just call him back up to duty on a carrier or sea tender.

The officer explained to Bob that the TAR program was an arm of the reserves where you were permanently based in one spot and that it was similar to the navy. Bob knew that TAR was a support system for the navy; it provided administrative and training support as well as support for operational matters, but he wasn't sold on the idea. He remembered how he ended up in the navy in the first place, being duped when he thought he had signed up for the Coast Guard.

The officer continued. "Bob, the base is located right on the other side of the field from Anacostia, between Anacostia and Bolling AFB. You can stay there until the program ends or until your enlistment is up. I have a friend in TAR, and I will give him your name. His name is Buddy Barnes, and he is the chief mechanic," said the officer. "Go see him."

Turning this over in his mind, he said he would think about it.

Wanting to make a good decision, Bob looked up Buddy Barnes and went over to see him. He thought Buddy was a character, full of laughter and great ideas. The two instantly hit it off. Buddy told Bob that he was always looking for a good person to join his crew and took him over to meet the chief of the metal shop. A week later, Bob received orders to report to the other side of the field. It looked like the TAR program was going to work for him.

In order to make all this happen, Bob had to resign, get discharged, and then reenlist at the same time. This made him quite nervous, but in the end, it all worked out. It only took four days to accomplish all of this. It was a nail-biting event for several days for both him and Anne. While he was in limbo, he had to serve as a Military Police (MP) at night in Washington, DC. This was not a duty anyone favored, so he mostly hung out in coffee shops those four nights with the other MPs because they didn't want to be out on the street.

Bob found himself out of the navy and then right back in the navy as a full-time reservist in the TAR program.

It was 1945. As a bluejacket, he learned so many life lessons and skills that formed the man he was now. The Bluejacket name comes from the Civil War, paying homage to contributions to American history. The term refers to an enlisted or junior officer in the Navy who usually spends a lot of time at sea.

The navy shaped his view of life. He now wondered what new things he would learn in the future. There was a saying that there was a right way to do things, a wrong way, and the navy way. Bob learned the navy way, and it stuck with him all his life.

Chapter 14

Enjoy the good times and keep your head up
during the bad times. Stay positive!
Your attitude will make or break you in the navy.

America's Navy

Moving to the TAR, renamed as Enlisted Surface Warfare Specialist (ESWS), was a good career move for Bob. A big plus was scoring a lot of airtime with his move, something he dreamed of since he was a boy flying high in the tamarack tree in Calexico. He found he was flying about twelve hours a week.

His first Assignment was to maintain the airplanes as a metal smith, something he was comfortable with. Most of the officers stationed in the reserves were also required to log a certain amount of airtime each week. So, it was a good deal all the way around. Bob usually traveled with the pilots in squadrons.

Early one morning on one of his first flight days, he received instructions to join a pilot in a North American SNJ-4 on a short solo flight to Philadelphia. He did not know the pilot very well and hoped the pilot was a good one; he never really knew what to expect. Personality and character as well as experience were vastly different between pilots. Bob climbed into the cockpit and buckled up. They took off from Anacostia and flew out over the Chesapeake Bay; they were supposed to circle the bay and then come back in for the landing.

On their way back, about half a mile from the runway, the engine sputtered and stopped dead. He watched as the pilot tried everything he could to get the engine started, but nothing worked. Luckily, the pilot showed some grit and experience and finally landed the plane with a hard bump. He was scared but gave thanks he was safe and not in a fiery heap somewhere.

The next week, Bob was on a flight to Cape May, New Jersey. This time there were two pilots in a Beechcraft twin-engine. He stood on the runway and eyed the pilots as they approached. They seemed comfortable with each other and were joking around, maybe a little too much, and Bob felt they should take the flight a little more seriously, especially after his experience the week before. He knew that when you get too cocky, you can overlook the details, and that can get you into trouble quick. He and the pilots greeted each other with a nod.

Bob sat directly behind the pilots and watched them read the daily newspaper. This made him a little nervous, so he kept his eyes glued on the instrument panel. When the plane was up about 11,000 feet, there was a loud pop, and everything on the plane went dead. It was eerily quiet, and Bob knew the engines stopped. He thought about that hard landing the week before and knew that at this altitude, the landing was not going to be just a hard bump.

The pilots scrambled to attention as their newspapers went flying everywhere. Bob watched as the copilot grabbled the wobble pump, trying to pump gas into the airplane. That did the trick, but it was a close call. When he had been watching the panel while the pilots read the paper, he had noticed the needle on the fuel tank drop very low. His role was strictly an observer on the flight, and he had been taught over and over to never question the pilot. From that moment on, he decided he would never hesitate to speak up if he saw something wrong. He figured they could yell at him later; at least he would be alive!

The navy was not the only military units stationed at Anacostia, and Bob learned to work alongside many different men, including the Marines assigned to the metal shop. Without too many mishaps but a lot of pranking, a friendly competition started between the two groups of men. The Marines serviced their own airplanes, and the navy did the same, but they were both eyeing how each other approached their work. Once, the Marines were assigned to repair a plane with a busted tail wheel. They had been at work for about six months on this one project. When finished, they finally took it outside to start it up. Everyone went out to watch. As soon as it started and began to roll, the wheel fell off again. It turns out the Marines twisted the hydraulics and installed them in reverse. There were a lot of laughs and guffaws before the Marines could live that down.

One morning, one of the Marines showed up to work with some girls in his car. Bob and about every man in the building looked out their window at them. When he was in San Diego, he had heard there were women working in the navy—WAVES they were called—but he had never met any. Now there were several stationed at his base! How the Marines convinced them to carpool, he didn't know, but this just led to more teasing between the two groups.

One afternoon, Bob and his friends took large sheets of paper, wrinkled them, and spray-painted the paper to match it to the Marine's car; they felt he was doing more than his share of carpooling. From the window of the Marine's office on the second floor, it looked like someone had scratched up the entire side of his car. The Marine looked out the window and blasted out of his office. Bob and his friends hid and watched him as he ran out of the building screaming mad. It wasn't until the Marine got right beside his car that he saw it was a joke. The Marine let them know he did not find in humor in the joke.

Another time, someone tied the axel of the Marine's parked car to the train track. When the WAVES came out and jumped in the car for their ride home, the car would not move. It took a long time for him to figure out what was wrong. No one ever admitted doing it, but the two groups eyed each other a little more closely going forward.

Bob's family was starting to grow. Anne and Bob had two daughters by now. He began looking for side work to support his family. He would stay late and tackle some side jobs in the electronic shop and also took on a private job in a television repair shop in Alexandria, Virginia. It was post war, and the booming years of radio and radar technology were just beginning. There was a high demand for TV repair. Every house wanted to have a big TV antenna mounted on their roof. Bob enjoyed the side work and especially liked the extra money!

Eventually, an opportunity came up at the base for Bob to work more in electronics. As Bob worked late one night, a station commander caught him working on a television in the shop.

The commander didn't recognize Bob. "Hey, are you new to the shop?" he asked, stopping at Bob's workstation.

"No, I am actually in the metal shop, but I am here doing some work on a TV that someone asked me to fix. I enjoy doing the work, and I only work on small projects when my other responsibilities are finished." Bob wasn't too sure if he was in trouble or what, so he didn't want to make any waves with the commander.

The commander stared him down and then smiled. "Well, son, you look like you know what you are doing. Would you like to come down here and work for me? I have a few openings, and I sure could use you." He paused and then continued. "If you agree, I will talk to your commander about a transfer."

Bob knew he was getting tired of the metal shop and his interest was turning more and more toward electronics, so he spoke up quickly, "Yes, sir, I would like a change, and I enjoy this type of work."

The next thing he knew, he was transferred to the radio shop. It was hard at first because he did not know any of the men who worked in radio. Radios and radar were new fields in aviation, and not many had the skills or knew how to use either. The commander could see in a short time that Bob had a knack for radios, so he was sent to school for training. He spent the next three years in training school. It changed the course of his work as much as the use of radar changed the destiny of aviation. Bob noticed that some of the men in the radio shop seemed to resent him. He thought this was so because of his specialized training but he decided to not let it bother him. In his training, he learned advanced radar and electronics as well as fire control and theory. There was lots of opportunity. Soon after he finished his training, the commander came to visit him while he was working in the radio shop.

"Bob, we are going to set up a new shop. It is only going to be for radar and aviation electronics," said the commander. "I would like to know if you would set up and manage the shop."

Bob knew that planes were being installed with advanced radar, and the field of aviation electronics was growing by leaps and bounds. "I would love to do that, sir!" he answered.

It took a year to set up his shop, but he knew it was well worth it to put in the time to produce a quality shop. Under the commander's guidance, Bob designed and configured what was referred to as confidential equipment, anti-submarine warfare, and other specialized equipment. He worked day and night on this along with his other side jobs, and finally he asked for some help in the shop. They assigned Bob an assistant, Henson, who proved to be smart and a speedy learner.

Even though Bob maintained the radio shop and added a few more men along the way, he was still required to put in flight time. This was a big plus for Bob! It gave him a break, and he loved to fly.

Bob was assigned to join a squadron flight to Africa. He was to support the electronics on the plane, and Bob's knowledge was put to the test. Before they took off, the crew was working on the electronics, but the pilot was in a hurry. He told them to wrap it up so they could get in the air.

It was pouring rain and frigid. The pilot gave them one hour and then they had to leave whether they were finished or not. Bob assured them that everything would be fine because they had just replaced the battery, but for some reason, the aircraft control system instrument panel would just not work. Bob and his crew took the wire off the battery and ran into the hangar to check it one more time. He saw the neon light was working, so he knew it was transmitting with no problem. He decided it must be the antennae. He ran back to the plane while the battery was being reinstalled. In the pouring rain, Bob climbed up through the hatch, trying to grab the antennae. He was wiping it down in a hurry and felt what seemed to be tape wrapped around it. Someone had broken the antennae and taped it back together! Bob hollered to a crewmate to run and get another one from the hanger. The pilot took off amid flashing lightening while Bob was screwing the antenna in place!

When they reached Casablanca, Bob was asked to teach the French how to use the radar in the same type of plane he flew in on. Bob discovered he enjoyed teaching the men and felt he was making a difference. Even though language was sometimes an issue, he was patient and did an excellent job.

On the return trip home, Bob ran the high frequency wire underneath the plane because communication was clearer. When the pilot did not need the communication for a while, Bob rolled it up like a fishing reel. As they were flying over Boston, he tried to roll it up and heard a loud thump. Then the wire would not pull. His guess was the wire was stuck. He felt like he had a fishing rod that had that had a lead elephant on the end of it to hold it down. Bob, doing what every good fisherman does, yanked it hard, and the line broke. It thundered down and took the reel with it. Bob didn't know where it landed, but he prayed it was not on a person!

Bob's new responsibilities included training on radar use. Just as he did with the French, from time to time, he would be sent a trainee, and he would partner with a pilot to give the trainee seat time as they learned how to use the radar. Bob would sit in the radar seat at first, and then he would switch with the trainee to let him have a hand at it.

By then, the navy had moved on from the TBM single-engine turbo prop to SP-2E and SP-2F Neptune aircraft and a variety of others. His favorite pilot was Buddy Barnes, who became one of his lifelong friends.

Bob was scheduled one weekend to train with Buddy as pilot, but both he and Buddy had plans for the weekend with their families and decided to find replacements. It was easy for Buddy to find a pilot to take his spot, but it was more difficult for Bob. Not everyone had his expertise. He asked around and then found a guy from his shop to trade duties with him. He also gave him a little money to sweeten the deal. The training was at an airfield near Chincoteague, Virginia. While Bob's replacement was working with the trainee on the radar, the tower was trying to radio the pilot that the plane's back right engine was smoking badly. Sometimes pilots got so engrossed with what was going on in the training sessions they forgot to keep an eye on the instrument panel. The plane was coming in for the landing and suddenly exploded. Everyone on the plane was killed. Two pilots and two airmen were on the plane. When Bob heard about this, he immediately blanched and thought, "That should have been me!" Bob and Buddy both had a hard time knowing that they both should have been on the plane.

To gain flight time, Bob would sometimes fly with a pilot over the Chesapeake Bay and practice dive-bombing on sailboats. He joined the same pilot each time for this training run. The pilot would play music in the cockpit, and when he was going in for a dive, he would turn the music way up. Straight down they would go, roll over, and then pull up. The pilot always waited until they were almost at the mast of the sailboat before pulling up. Affected by the extreme g-forces, Bob would often gray out, and it was difficult to get his head up to see what was going on around him. Bob did not care; he loved the thrill of the whole maneuver. Bob would lie in bed at night reliving the flight and going over the memories of each twist and tune.

Bob's radio shop grew and grew with all the new technology pouring in daily. He requested and added more positions. His shop was thriving, and he built an excellent reputation. It was through this new position that Bob finally earned his title of first class chief petty officer. Bob was no longer a bluejacket and had entered the rank of officer. He was so proud that he had come this far. He had left high school before his senior year, received his GED through the navy, and now he was an officer!

When you think about it, this is the way Bob lived his life. He was always ready for a new opportunity. He learned quickly and worked hard. He learned from his life experiences and kept moving forward. Bob, born during the Great Depression, developed character at the 101 Ranch, courage at Pearl Harbor, and integrity as a frontier man diving into the Cold War's technological advances in aviation, electronics, and radar technology.

Chapter 15

It is said that your life flashes before your eyes just before you die.
That is true, it is called Life.

Terry Pratchett

The hospital room was dimly lit as Bob lay quietly in bed listening to the murmurs of voices in the hall. He had his headset on and was listening to Benny Goodman and tunes from the forties. He knew he was in the ICU where, after struggling with a raging fever the week before, he was still trying to get better.

He had time on his hands to reflect on his life, reliving the dusty days of life in the California desert to Oklahoma mucking the stall of the black-and-white palomino and watching trick cowboys who eventually became Hollywood heroes. He struggled through memories as his relived his experience at Pearl Harbor when he forcefully became a man at the mere age of seventeen as he watched wartime at its worst.

He reflected on his years of service in the navy and knew he could not complain. After twenty years, three months, and six days of active duty, he could only recall growth and knowledge under its leadership. In August 1960, he moved on to civilian life in the field he loved by accepting a position with the Federal Aviation

Administration (FAA). Bob was proud to be hired as an aviation technician, GS-11. The FAA was two years young when he was hired, and he worked right in the heart of Washington, DC.

He looked around the room and knew he was in the Oklahoma Hospital in the city he now called home with his second wife. For most of his adult life, he called Northern Virginia his home and lived just outside of Washington, DC, in the suburbs of Fairfax and Arlington.

He thought about his first wife, Anne. He met Anne in Washington, DC, on a trolley ride, and together they raised three daughters and a son. He was a forward thinker and supported Anne's desire for a career of her own.

Now, as a man in his late eighties and almost ninety, he was glad that he had reconnected with his children, developing new relationships with them in recent years. When Bob moved to Oklahoma City, he moved away from his children living in Northern Virginia. He was no longer in close contact with them. The children remained close to their mother in distance and in everyday life. Bob remarried and adjusted to life with his new wife and her family. His children only saw him on brief visits.

The voices in the hallway were getting a little louder, and his thoughts turned toward his more recent work that brought him to Oklahoma City. Toward the end of his career with the FAA, he transferred to Oklahoma City as part of aircraft program activities. He was assigned first to Flight Inspection as a GS-14, and later he oversaw the restoration of the FAA's DC-3. He was then assigned as manager of the FAA DC-3 Aircraft Airshow Program. He initiated and managed the DC-3 program until he retired in June 1988, with a total government service of forty-eight years and a few weeks.

Several years before moving permanently to Oklahoma City, he and Anne tried a long-distance relationship, and he frequently traveled back and forth to Virginia, but that failed, and they grew apart during these years. After their divorce, he soon remarried, building a new life with a woman who worked in his department in the Oklahoma field office.

A nurse glanced in the room, and Bob pretended he was asleep. He never liked the hospital, and he didn't like them poking at him. As he closed his eyes, he recounted his life in retirement. He enjoyed his career years embracing the cutting edge of technology in jet aviation, radar, and electronics. He wished he could fly one more time in one of the cockpits with the pilots.

Now that he was retired, he had time to do the things he enjoyed but never had time for, like fishing, visiting the grandkids, or attending Pearl Harbor reunions to share his experiences. Most of all, he worked in his garden and shop in his backyard. He loved to rebuild old radios and practiced computerized flying simulators. He closed his eyes tight and hung on the memory of the simulators. He was the pilot in the simulators, and he could close his eyes to hear the plane's motor and imagine feeling the wind rushing by the windows to relive his years in the cockpit.

After dozing for a few minutes, Bob awoke, startled. Looking again around the room and realizing his circumstances, he instinctively knew what had happened. One afternoon while showering, he was bit by several mosquitos while washing off the dirt from working in the garden. In the shower, he slapped at the insects and then glanced at the torn screen in the bathroom window. He remembered he placed a bucket of standing water just below the window in the yard. He reminded himself he needed to dispose of the standing water. This was something he had been meaning to do for a while, but he always seemed to forget.

A week later, he started showing signs of the flu but went about his days taking aspirin to keep away the mild aches and fever. He was not one to spend a sick day in bed and refused to admit he was sick. He finally succumbed to the point where his wife had to call the rescue squad. The EMTs had a difficult time convincing him to go to the hospital. Bob despised the hospital because it reminded him of the dead men stacked in the mess hall during the Pearl Harbor attack. He believed if he went to the hospital he would never come back home.

After a couple of days, Bob began to feel better and was moved out of ICU. He was often caught joking with the staff. One morning while the doctors were visiting him, he asked if he could have some of those little pills his doctor gave him. The doctors, skeptical, asked, "Mr. Barrigan, what kind of pills?"

"You know," Bob laughed, "those pills that Rush Limbaugh takes."

Bob found out that Rush Limbaugh's doctor prescribed oxycodone for him to help with his arthritic knee pain. Rush Limbaugh was a popular political commentator and radio personality who was once arrested on drug prescription charges. The doctors laughed and told him they had something better. As he continued to slowly improve, he teased the nurses constantly, promising them that when he got out, he would buy them bikes, clothes, and anything they wanted.

During this time, two of his daughters stopped by to visit him. They stayed for several days until they were told they could go home and that their dad was out of the woods. Before his daughters left, the CDC confirmed that a mosquito carrying the West Nile virus had bitten him. He contracted West Nile virus, which, in turn, caused a weakened immune system, opening the door for encephalitis.

Even though he was in good spirits, Bob thought about how this just might be the end for him. Despite feeling better, there was no mention about him going home. As he continued to reflect upon his life, he felt he lived a good one. He started out poor and worked hard, always reaching for that next experience. He provided well for his family and was always kind to them. He didn't want to die, but he felt he needed to take stock of his life.

One evening when his daughters were preparing to fly back to their homes on the East Coast, he asked them to sit and talk with him awhile.

"I know you are headed to your homes, but I have a favor to ask of you," Bob said as he sat up in bed.

Eileen placed her hand on his shoulder. "OK! Do you want need anything? Do you want us to bring you some more music?"

"No, this is about your mother. Now listen to me." Bob paused for a moment because he wanted his request to be straightforward, and it was difficult to talk. "My wife has always been good to me, I love her deeply, and we have a good life here. But your mother, she was the love of my life." He paused as he thought about how that might sound. "Do you understand what I am saying?" he asked softly.

He continued. "I was thinking I never went to her funeral or talked to her when she was really sick. When I die, I don't want to see her in the hereafter without flowers in my hand. When that time comes, will you go to her grave and put some yellow roses on it with a note that they are from me?"

With tears in her eyes, Julie responded softly, "We can do that, Dad. We will place flowers on her grave with a note."

Eileen nodded in agreement and said, "You won't see her again empty-handed. No worries."

Bob added, pointing a finger at them, "And go home and dump any standing water that is in your yards!"

The girls hugged their father and flew home the following day. Soon after that time, Bob was visited by his son and grandchildren and was released to a rehabilitation facility. A couple of weeks later, he passed peacefully in his sleep on September 17, 2013. He was eighty-nine years old.

Epilogue

America without her soldiers
would be like God without His angels.

Claudia Pemberton

The car drove slowly across the bridge and parked to the right of the paved path at the entrance to the cemetery. Bob's daughters, Eileen and Julie, exited the car and detoured into the visitor center to pick up a map. Though there were people milling through the park, there was a somber silence that hung heavy in the air. The two women could hear birds singing and quiet whispers of visitors carrying on the soft breeze. It was peaceful.

They linked their arms at the elbow and slowly walked down the paved walkway, their heels clicking on the stone surface. Holding the park map they simultaneously saw the headstone sitting underneath a golden maple tree.

Together, the two women stood at their father's grave. Eileen was holding a single yellow rose. Speaking for both sisters, she explained to her father that they finally understood the value and impact he had had on their lives.

She continued, "This is a good resting place for you in Arlington Cemetery. You are surrounded by some of the men and women that grew up in your time, shared your experiences, and even served alongside you."

Passing the rose to her sister, Julie told their father how they had honored his request and how they placed flowers on their mother's grave. Smiling, Julie told him that they were sure he met their mother in Heaven with flowers in his hand.

Kneeling, Bob's daughters, with tears brightening in their eyes, placed the single rose on his grave.

"We miss you," Eileen tenderly added.

About the Authors

J ulie Boyd and Eileen Lockhart are sisters who were born in the suburbs of Washington, D. C. Julie resides in Virginia Beach, Virginia, near her two sons and four grandsons. She is a retired elementary school principal from Loudoun County, Virginia. She is presently a reiki master who loves music and is an avid reader. She is the published author of *Heart Ribbons*.

Eileen resides with her husband on a small farm in Woodford, Virginia. She has a son who lives in Scotland with his wife and child, and a daughter who lives in Washington State with her husband and three children. Eileen is presently the professional development coordinator for Prince William County Schools in Virginia. Eileen serves as an adjunct professor at local universities. In her spare time, she is a travel agent with her own company, Never Ending World Travel.

CPSIA information can be obtained
at www.ICGtesting.com
Printed in the USA
JSHW072125190123
36466JS00007B/117

9 781685 150846